Tooting Your Own Horn:

Web-Based Public Relations for the 21st Century Librarian

Ann Hill and Julieta Dias Fisher

Linworth
PUBLISHING, INC

To our wonderful children:

Joscelyn, Ian, Marcie, Don, Matthew, and Kerry.

Their love and support are so important to us.

Library of Congress Cataloging-in-Publication Data

Hill, Ann, 1947-
    Tooting your own horn: web-based public relations for the 21st century librarian / Ann
Hill and Julieta Dias Fisher.
        p. cm.
    Includes bibliographical references and index.
    ISBN 1-58683-066-X (perfectbound)
    1. Libraries--Public relations. 2. Library Web sites--Design. 3. Internet in public
relations. I. Fisher, Julieta Dias. II. Title.

Z716.3 .H45 2003
021.7--dc21   2002032440

Published by Linworth Publishing, Inc.
480 East Wilson Bridge Road, Suite L
Worthington, Ohio 43085

Copyright © 2002 by Linworth Publishing, Inc.

ISBN: 1-58683-066-X

5 4 3 2 1

Table of Contents

Acknowledgements

We wish to express our appreciation to several people who assisted us in writing this book: Peter Dahlgren for his insightful suggestions, comments, and unwavering support; Joscelyn Fisher, Ian Fisher, Mary Hayko, and Don and Marcie Pullano for their enthusiastic encouragement and constructive criticism; Nicholas Gasparovich for technical assistance; and Judi Repman for all of her editorial help, her encouragement, and for responding to our countless e-mails.

Introduction

Many librarians have been transformed into cybrarians, using the Internet to provide information to students, teachers, administrators, parents, and the community. Creating a home page transforms your brick-and-mortar building into a virtual library without walls, providing limitless access to the library and its resources. At the same time, a home page showcases the library program not only in the school, but also in the district and the community.

This how-to manual was developed in response to an article, "Showcasing your Library via a Home Page," published in *The Book Report*, and workshops given for New Jersey librarians and media specialists at the annual Educational Media Association convention and to teachers at the New Jersey National Education Association convention. The reaction to the article and the workshops was overwhelming. We were inundated with e-mail from librarians asking us about our home page and its content. We realized that there were articles in professional journals on the need for an "electronic presence" for libraries, but there were no books written on this subject. As a result, we knew that librarians needed a how-to manual to assist them in transforming traditional marketing programs into a Web-based marketing tool. In fact, this manual is one of the first books on using a home page for marketing libraries.

Since there is no definitive work on using the power of a home page to publicize the services of the library, this book, though aimed at media specialists, can also be adapted to suit other types of librarians who want to establish a digital presence for their library.

This book offers a step-by-step approach to marketing your program and offers innovative promotional ideas to showcase your library. There are three caveats to using this book. First, start small. There are not enough hours in your already busy schedule to implement all of the ideas in this book. The book's organization allows you to focus on ideas that meet your library's program needs. Start with the marketing ideas that will provide the most visibility for your library. Second, the ideas presented in this book are a jumping-off point for your marketing program. They can be adapted to suit your library and its program. Third, examples of home pages created by librarians in Australia, Canada, and the United States are included to illustrate each marketing idea included in the book. The home pages are representative examples and by no means the only examples of ways found on the Internet to market your library program.

This book is divided into eight chapters and includes an index, bibliography, and glossary. Each chapter includes descriptions, planning advice, design considerations, and examples for each marketing idea. Sample forms, surveys, Web sites, and resources are also included.

Chapter One provides an overview of public relations for the 21st century librarian. It focuses on the importance of a well-planned public relations program in the Information Age and the use of a home page to implement it.

Chapter Two examines the teacher collaborative process. It shows how a home page can become a crucial resource in teacher planning and professional development, and how the services provided on the home page will enhance the teacher-librarian collaborative process.

Chapter Three provides marketing ideas that will make your students fans of the library. It shows various ways to transform traditional information literacy programs into Web-based services. It also looks at ways to actively involve students in the library program though a student advisory board and the creation of home pages. Finally, it outlines ways that a home page can highlight student achievement and creativity.

Chapter Four focuses on services that the school library can offer to the community via a home page. These services break down the barriers between the school and the community as its members access and use the resources of the virtual library.

Chapter Five highlights promotional strategies. This chapter outlines ideas that can be used to virtually showcase your library and its resources to teachers, staff, and students on an ongoing basis. It includes how-to tips on the technical aspects of converting print promotional materials into an electronic format.

Chapter Six focuses on special events and expands upon the ideas introduced in Chapter Five. This includes examples of special events that can be used to publicize your program to a larger audience.

Chapter Seven highlights reading promotion. It describes innovative ideas to encourage reading throughout the school as well as common reading projects that can be adapted to a home page.

The book concludes with Chapter Eight, which briefly summarizes the previous chapters and advises librarians to be knowledgeable about technology policies governing their specific libraries before they begin to design their home pages.

Implementing a marketing program using a home page is not difficult. Any librarian can duplicate or adapt the ideas found in this how-to manual. It just requires time, planning, and dedication. The reward is a home page that results in higher visibility for your program in your school and in the community.

Chapter One

Public Relations for the 21st Century Library

Introduction

Many librarians are notorious for their modesty; hence, they are reluctant to toot their own horn. However, publicity is paramount to alert people to your program. The success of a library program depends on librarians and the partnerships they build with teachers, students, and those who hold the purse strings—administrators, board members, and parents. Public relations is especially important during tight economic times when these people scrutinize how and where each dollar is being spent. Whereas public libraries compete with other government agencies, school libraries compete for funding between district buildings and other school programs such as band and athletics. Therefore, it is imperative to let students, faculty, administrators, and the community know what you are offering so they will be aware of your program. For example, you may have a special program for senior citizens or an interesting book club; their visibility, publicity, and functionality on a home page allow these activities to flourish and succeed. Because there are more working parents today and their work schedules conflict with school scheduling, many parents cannot find the time to attend school conferences or communicate with their children's teachers. A home page provides a much-needed link between the school and the parent. Through e-mail and access to a library home page, parents can be instantly apprised of what teachers expect, as well as the services that the library provides.

Information Power: Building Partnerships for Learning (American Association of School Librarians and Association for Educational Communications and Technology, 1998), also fondly known as the librarian's bible, states that no individual school contains all the resources and information that students need to master to flourish in the 21st century. As increasing numbers of schools and homes connect to global information services, media specialists, along with classroom teachers, can electronically communicate directly with parents in order to involve them in students' learning experiences and to provide information about their children's needs and progress (128–129).

According to Eric Newburger in *Home Computers and Internet Use in the United States: August 2000*, Internet usage has more than doubled in the past two years across all age groups, from 22.8% in 1998 to 47.4% in 2000. In 2001 98% of schools were connected to the Internet. In 2000, 65% of children ages 3–17 had Internet connection at home, an increase of 55% from that in 1998. More than half of school age children had access to computers in school as well as at home. The survey found only 10.4% of school age children with no Internet access at all. For many children with no Internet access at home, schools provide this access. Thus, most estimates indicate that over half of the U.S. population uses the Internet, suggesting that the "digital divide" is definitely shrinking not only in the United States, but also throughout the world. According to a February 2002 survey, "How Many Online," conducted by NUA.com, an online source for Internet demographics and surveys, there are 544.4 million Internet users worldwide. Because widespread access to the Internet has brought increasing familiarity and proficiency, both teachers and students are becoming more comfortable with the new technology and find it easier to use the Internet rather than traditional print media. For many children who have been exposed to computers since early childhood, clicking and pointing is just as natural as breathing, consequently making them receptive to Web-related ideas and projects. The more people use computers for games, news updates, consumer needs, and general research, the more proficient they become. Due to this ease of use and consequent familiarity, librarians must take advantage of the Internet's ability to reach a vast number of people. It took 38 years for radio to reach 50 million American homes, 12 years for television to reach the same number and only four years for the World Wide Web to make its presence known (Newburger). This proliferation of communication technology has had staggering implications for education, entertainment, and commerce.

The prevalence of the Internet is captured in Ed Stein's wonderful 1996 cartoon in *The Rocky Mountain News* (see Figure 1.1).

Impact of a Home Page as a Public Relations Tool

Millions of users log on to the Internet every day to access digitized information available globally 24 hours a day. Because the Internet is such a tremendous communications vehicle, promotional methods that were acceptable to business 10 years ago are no longer viable and many companies are forgoing traditional public relations. They have switched from communicating via press releases through journalists to spinning their own messages directly online and through e-mail. According to the U.S. Census Bureau statistics, retail e-commerce sales were up 8.3% in 2001 from the same third quarter in 2000.

The global reach of the Internet has forced businesses to keep up technologically to stay competitive. Since everybody uses the Web, potential customers who do not see a company online will not recognize the company as established unless it has a virtual presence, thus forcing more and more companies to establish themselves on the Internet in order to stay competitive. Internet e-commerce has become the underpinning for all successful businesses. A home page not only becomes a more efficient equivalent to an ad in a newspaper, but its global reach and interactive capabilities makes it a more effective form of advertising. Unlike a static advertisement, you can tell how many times the home page has been accessed and what, if anything, needs to be done to improve it by asking for feedback via the e-mail link on the home page. In fact, most companies prefer to use e-mail rather than letters or faxes, as it is quicker and more convenient.

Home pages also allow public relations professionals to do their job of influencing the public without spending an enormous amount of money on traditional advertising and promotions. This makes promotion via a home page a boon to small companies who cannot afford to have a public relations company advertise their business, so businesses can promote themselves. This virtual presence and location is just as important to libraries and the promotion of library programs. School libraries can target and reach their audience in the same way as the business community attracts its customers.

Jim Fleck, a specialist in marketing libraries, says in *The Wizard's Media Handbook: Profitably Promoting Your Library With the Media*, "the information marketplace is so crowded with new and improved brilliant technological innovations, that libraries have seemed to become invisible, some even fear that they are on the verge of obsolescence and maybe extinction" (3). How many times have librarians heard that they and their libraries will soon be obsolete now that the Internet provides all the information society needs? In actuality, the Internet does provide information, but it is not adequate for multilayered queries or in-depth research. In order to correct the misperception of libraries staffed by dusty, old, nearsighted librarians that sit in dim corners zealously guarding their tomes, we need to promote ourselves as information specialists and broaden the scope of our services to stay abreast with technological developments. Fleck says, "we need to learn how to promote the library utilizing the same media tools that other businesses have utilized so well. Our communities must see and hear that libraries are easily accessible and progressive and most importantly they belong to us" (3).

Public Relations in the School Library

Public relations and promotion is an important part of communicating your program to the general population both in school and in the community. This is especially important when it comes to school administrators and board members. If they are unaware of what you are doing or what your program entails, they cannot and will not be supportive of you. Therefore, it is important to publicize your program to them via newsletters, meetings, and news blurbs. With technology, all of these library-marketing strategies can be encapsulated into a home page. A recent *Book Report* article by Steven Baule and Laura Bertani, "Marketing 101 for Your Library Media Program" (2000) makes a strong case for marketing when they say "promote your program on the Web by creating a Web page for your school library program. E-commerce is the way of the future" (48). In the past, community relationships and programs had to be scheduled to suit the librarian and the organizations. With a home page there are no time constraints, as one librarian can be in many places at one time, simultaneously giving workshops, conducting meetings, interacting with students or faculty, all with a click of the mouse. Having a home page is also an asset for students whose busy lives do not allow for time to use the library during the school day. The home page enables them to peruse the library's databases and Web links at any time of the day or night.

Just as technology has transformed traditional and tedious library functions such as cataloging and circulation procedures into faster and more efficient services, it has also given librarians a vehicle to communicate and disseminate information in an efficient way to students and faculty. *Information Power: Building Partnerships for Learning* asserts that "collaboration, leadership, and technology underline *Information Power* and the vision of a dynamic, student-centered library media program that begins in the school and extends its connections throughout the community, the nation, and the world" (130).

Forging these connections requires outreach and advocacy, which are no longer limited by traditional print methods of reaching the community. Physical considerations and time limitations no longer hamper outreach because technological developments allow an electronic global presence via a home page. It is the newest method to creatively promote and showcase your program as it offers the school and the community instant access to a library 24 hours a day, seven days a week. In order to stay current with technological developments, it is essential for a library in the 21st century to have a virtual or electronic presence throughout the school and community. Once the home page is accessed and used, it becomes the principal communication tool between the library and its users.

A home page can garner support for your program by projecting an effective school library image that targets not only the community within the school, but also those outside the school walls by making information easily accessible. This requires innovative and creative planning and a proactive attitude. A strong Madison Avenue marketing campaign of creating a product and then promoting it is paramount here. First, grab the users' attention by creating a home page that is visually inviting and easy to use. Then inform them of the services offered on it through e-mails and newsletters.

Lisa Wolfe in *Library Public Relations, Promotions & Communications: a How-to-Do-it Manual* (1997) recommends having "at least one person devoted to public relations" (3). While many academic and school libraries can utilize their public relations office for promotion and large city public libraries can afford a public relations staff, many libraries do not have the available funds for this type of service. The Internet is an efficient resource for libraries that do not have a centralized public relations department or a public relations person. A home page, though time consuming at first, can resolve many of the public relations dilemmas for these types of libraries.

Traditionally, the library marketed itself by alerting its clientele of its programs, such as hours of operation, children's programming, and other events. In order to thrive in today's information-competitive environment, librarians must not only build on these traditions, but also adapt to an ever-changing environment. To stay viable, the library's community has to be fully informed of not only what the library provides, but also how its services can enhance daily life. Promoting your library can be accomplished by creating a home page that shows teachers and students how invaluable the library is, and makes them wonder how they ever survived without these shortcuts before. Soon you will not only be barraged with e-mail for Webquests and other types of teacher collaboration, but teachers will tell other teachers of this wonderful service, thus adding to your visibility. Foster good community relationships by promoting special events in the community. When members of the community spread the word about the good programs in the library, you know that your library is making an impact. Word of mouth is the best promotion in any field of endeavor.

Needs Assessment

When you start to design and add content to your home page, it may seem overwhelming. No home page can provide all possible informational sources without making the page cluttered and difficult to read and access. All libraries, whether they are academic, public, school, or special libraries, have much in common. They all subscribe to the *Library Bill of Rights* and they all adhere to the basic philosophy of service to their clientele. However, there are very few libraries that can be all things to all people. Once the clientele's needs are identified, then the appropriate program can be designed to serve their needs.

Therefore, it is a good idea to tailor your home page to the select audience of each community. You can do this by surveys to students, faculty, and community members. Once you have established your home page, post these surveys on your home page to encourage a two-way flow of information.

This interaction between the library and its members is important for planning and for making students and faculty feel that the library is theirs. Creating pride and ownership in a library and its programs takes planning, action, and collaboration between the library staff and the community it serves. Social scientists have conducted many studies on the impact of cooperation, competition, and independence, which indicate that cooperative teamwork rather than competitive or independent stances is more viable for a successful program. When people are involved with the process, they are more apt to have a sense of "ownership" of their library.

Location of Surveys

There are many ways to determine the needs of a community. One method is through use of annual needs assessments sent to students and staff members for suggestions on how to improve library services.

There are various places on your home page to locate needs assessments as well as other surveys and forms. You could have a category on your home page entitled surveys and forms. Include forms and letters that have been sent home from school that parents can access if they have been mislaid. Also include tax and legal forms as well as all surveys within this section. You can also locate the surveys and forms in different sections within your home page. For example, locate student surveys on the teacher assignment page. Students can fill out the survey after a class research project in the library. Locate teacher surveys on the professional development page, which teachers can submit at their leisure or after completion of a class project. Parents can complete their survey during back-to-school night after taking a virtual tour of the library or at a PTA meeting. Place the public librarians' survey on the community outreach section of the home page. Surveys have a limited virtual life, so set a time frame for their completion.

The following are surveys, (see Figures 1.2, 1.3, 1.4, 1.5), which can be adapted to individual libraries.

Figure 1.2   Teacher Survey

When surveying the faculty you need to ascertain how individual teachers use the library. Do they use it for research by small groups or by individuals? Are their needs being met and if not, how can services be improved?

Figure 1.3   Student Survey

It is always important to receive input from students to determine when they use the library. Receiving feedback on these services can be both informative and humorous. Perhaps you will find that your school has many non-users and those that are faithful users believe that offering cappuccino and chocolate cake will make for a perfect library!

Figure 1.4   Parent Survey

A survey will advertise your services to parents and, at the same time, garner feedback about their knowledge of the library's programs and services.

Figure 1.5   Public Library Survey

Last, but certainly not least, it is important to collaborate with your public library. You need to determine how often your students use the public library and how effective your informational skills program is outside the school library setting. This survey is e-mailed to the public library in your community.

Disseminating surveys is an efficient method to gauge community needs and perceptions. Based on the data that is collected after your surveys, you will be able to identify the various needs that can be met through the establishment of a home page for your school library.

Figure 1.2 Teacher Survey

Teacher Survey

I use the library for the following: (Check all that apply.)

- [ ] I bring my class
- [ ] I send small groups of students
- [ ] I send individual students
- [ ] I allow students to utilize before or after school library hours
- [ ] I allow students to visit during their study halls
- [ ] I send students to visit during lunch
- [ ] I come on my own

Please evaluate our library program.

Your students' perceptions of the library
◉ Excellent ◉ Good ◉ Fair ◉ Poor

Rate your overall working relationship with the library
◉ Excellent ◉ Good ◉ Fair ◉ Poor

Staff is cooperative in helping you with your program
◉ Excellent ◉ Good ◉ Fair ◉ Poor

The library staff's willingness to assemble materials for projects and bibliographies
◉ Excellent ◉ Good ◉ Fair ◉ Poor

The librarians' efforts to keep abreast of what is going on in the classroom
◉ Excellent ◉ Good ◉ Fair ◉ Poor

Your efforts in keeping the librarians informed about what you are doing in your classroom
◉ Excellent ◉ Good ◉ Fair ◉ Poor

Adequacy of print materials for the subject at the grade level you teach
◉ Excellent ◉ Good ◉ Fair ◉ Poor

Adequacy of the non-print collection for the subject at the grade level you teach
◉ Excellent ◉ Good ◉ Fair ◉ Poor

Adequacy of the electronic databases for the subject and grade level you teach
◉ Excellent ◉ Good ◉ Fair ◉ Poor

Your satisfaction with the circulation policies for faculty
◉ Excellent ◉ Good ◉ Fair ◉ Poor

The librarians' collaboration with you in purchasing new material
◉ Excellent ◉ Good ◉ Fair ◉ Poor

Your success in locating materials
◉ Excellent ◉ Good ◉ Fair ◉ Poor

The effectiveness of the library in the academic sphere
◉ Excellent ◉ Good ◉ Fair ◉ Poor

General appearance of the library
◉ Excellent ◉ Good ◉ Fair ◉ Poor

Please comment on the following:

The best thing about our library program is

Our library program can be improved by

The collection is weak in the following areas:

Subject Area/Grade _____ Date _____

SUBMIT   CLEAR

Figure 1.3 Student Survey

Student Survey

In an effort for ongoing excellence, we would like you to complete this survey at your earliest convenience.
How often do you use the library?
  ◎ Four times a week   ◎ Twice a week   ◎ Once a week   ◎ Once a month
When do you use the library?
  ◎ Before school   ◎ During school   ◎ After school   ◎ All of these

---

Please rate the library's computers and online databases.
The Number of Computers
  ◎ Excellent   ◎ Good   ◎ Fair   ◎ Poor
Online Databases

Ebscohost	SIRS
◎ Excellent ◎ Good ◎ Fair ◎ Poor	◎ Excellent ◎ Good ◎ Fair ◎ Poor
Galenet	Wilson Web
◎ Excellent ◎ Good ◎ Fair ◎ Poor	◎ Excellent ◎ Good ◎ Fair ◎ Poor

---

Please tell us how often you use the library for the following things:

Complete homework or class assignments	Borrow T1 calculator link
◎ Frequently ◎ Sometimes ◎ Seldom ◎ Never	◎ Frequently ◎ Sometimes ◎ Seldom ◎ Never
Study	Borrow CDs
◎ Frequently ◎ Sometimes ◎ Seldom ◎ Never	◎ Frequently ◎ Sometimes ◎ Seldom ◎ Never
Research	Use the scanners
◎ Frequently ◎ Sometimes ◎ Seldom ◎ Never	◎ Frequently ◎ Sometimes ◎ Seldom ◎ Never
Borrow digital camera	Use Word, PowerPoint, Excel, and Publisher
◎ Frequently ◎ Sometimes ◎ Seldom ◎ Never	◎ Frequently ◎ Sometimes ◎ Seldom ◎ Never
Borrow books	Use the Internet
◎ Frequently ◎ Sometimes ◎ Seldom ◎ Never	◎ Frequently ◎ Sometimes ◎ Seldom ◎ Never
Borrow laptop computer	Meeting friends
◎ Frequently ◎ Sometimes ◎ Seldom ◎ Never	◎ Frequently ◎ Sometimes ◎ Seldom ◎ Never
Borrow videos	
◎ Frequently ◎ Sometimes ◎ Seldom ◎ Never	

Please rate the library's staff.

Friendliness	Helpfulness
◎ Excellent ◎ Good ◎ Fair ◎ Poor	◎ Excellent ◎ Good ◎ Fair ◎ Poor

---

We would like you to comment on the following:
Have you tried to find books on certain subjects that are not included in our collection? If so, please list these subjects.

Have you found good Web sites that are not included on our home page? If so, please give us the URLs.

What do you like best about the library?   How can we improve our library?

Name

SUBMIT   CLEAR

Figure 1.4   Parent Survey

Parent Survey

In an effort for ongoing excellence, we would like you to complete this survey at your earliest convenience.

How often have you visited your child's school library this year?
◉ Once   ◉ Twice   ◉ Three or more times

Has your child ever needed to use other libraries to complete an assignment?
◉ Yes   ◉ No

Do you feel that the resources in our library are adequate for your child's needs?
◉ Yes   ◉ No

Do you assist your child with Internet research at home?
◉ Yes   ◉ No

Are you aware of the library's home page?
◉ Yes   ◉ No

Are you aware of Newbery (an annual award for the most distinguished contribution to children's literature) and Caldecott (an annual award for the most distinguished picture book for children) books?
◉ Yes   ◉ No

Do you have computer software at home to help children with schoolwork?
◉ Yes   ◉ No

Did you know that the library is available for your child during homeroom, study hall, lunch, after school, and during class time?
◉ Yes   ◉ No

Please suggest ways to help us assist your child.

SUBMIT   CLEAR

Figure 1.5 Public Library Survey

Public Library Survey

Please check the information sources that students use the most in your library.

Books/Periodicals
☐ Reference   ☐ Internet
☐ Online databases   ☐ E-mail

Study
Do students display effective research strategies when using the resources of the public library?
◉ Yes   ◉ No

In what research areas do students need improvement?

In what research areas are students most proficient?

Do students effectively communicate their research needs to the librarians?

What kinds of programs/workshops does the library offer?

Does the library offer any research databases? If so, please list them and comment on the frequency of student use.

Do you find that students would rather use the Internet and other technologies rather than print resources?

What percentage of patrons is comprised of students between the ages of 6 and 18?

List ways the school librarians can assist the public librarian.

SUBMIT   CLEAR

Setting Up a Home Page

In the movie *Field of Dreams*, the main character Ray Kinsella hears a voice that says, "If you build it, they will come." He builds a baseball field in the middle of an Iowa cornfield and somehow, without any promotion or advertising, hordes of fans suddenly appear. With libraries it's not that easy. A library can have the most beautiful facility, but if no one knows about it, it will remain an empty, beautiful facility. Take this analogy one step further; if you promote your library through a home page, they will come!

The goal is to make your home page the first place that teachers, students, and the community go to for information. Since librarians have so many responsibilities and so little time to implement new projects, the task of designing, organizing, and creating a home page may seem overwhelming at first; however, the effort involved will be well worth the investment. Once the page is established, the dividends will rise exponentially.

As you begin to design your home page, the first thing to do is to determine your audience. Once the audience has been determined and their needs identified, decide the content and design of your page and actually set it up! For example, some people may think that a lot of color and graphics are appropriate for an elementary library home page, but not for a high school home page, and yet others may disagree. It is all a matter of personal taste and opinion. Decide what type of message you want to convey. Do you want to add curriculum links, database brochures, Webquests, and newsletters for your students and teachers, or do you want to include the community and promote the library as an entertaining as well as an informative place by promoting special events and programs? The possibilities of the content of a home page are endless, from new arrivals of books and videos to virtual displays of special events and contests.

There are many books on the technical aspects of setting up a home page. You do not need to be expert in .HTML, (Hypertext Markup Language, the language usually used for creating home pages), as programs such as Microsoft FrontPage and Dreamweaver make it very easy. If you are hesitant about starting a home page yourself, there are various ways to go about creating one. The school computer club is a start or you can get library assistants to help you; many students are more than willing to show off their expertise. In fact, a student got us started on our home page five years ago. Our first efforts were very minimal, as we were not sure what we wanted to include on it or how to design it. But once we had an idea of what we wanted to portray, it was a fun and challenging task! Another way to establish a home page is to collaborate with the district Webmaster. If your district has a district Web page and a Webmaster, you can relegate that chore to him or her. Finally, you can get ideas from the home pages that already exist on the Internet. There are hundreds of impressive school library home pages on the Internet. As you sift through these, decide what you would like to incorporate into your home page and what would not work for your specific library. The following sites provide a directory of some schools and school libraries on the Web with excellent home pages. As you review them, bookmark the ones that appeal to you so that you can get ideas for your own home page.

School Directories on the Web

School Library Resources on the Internet
          <http://www.iasl-slo.org/>
Peter Milbury's Network of School Librarian Web Pages
          <http://www.school-libraries.net>

Some Exemplary Library Home Pages

Mt. Laurel's Hartford School in Mt. Laurel, New Jersey
          <http://38.139.53.3/mc/>
Barley Sheaf School Library in Flemington, New Jersey
          <http://www.frsd.k12.nj.us/barleylibrary/>
Springfield Township High School Virtual Library in Springfield Township,
     Pennsylvania
          < http://mciunix.mciu.k12.pa.us/~spjvweb/>
Senior Library, Scotch College in Melbourne, Australia
          <http://www.scotch.vic.edu.au/Library/library.htm>
Woodlands High School McCullough Campus Library, The Woodlands, Texas
          <http://info.conroe.isd.tenet.edu/senior/mccullough/
               TWHS-McClibrary/index.htm>
Mt. Erie Elementary School Library in Anacortes, Washington
          <http://mte.anacortes.k12.wa.us/library/library.htm>
Melbourne High School Library in Victoria, Australia
          <http://www.mhs.vic.edu.au/home/library/>
Geebung State School Library in Queensland, Australia
          <http://www.geebungss.qld.edu.au/glib.htm>
Athena Media Center in Rochester, New York
          <http://www.greece.k12.ny.us/ath/library/>
Oxnard High School Library Information Center in Oxnard, California
          <http://www.ouhsd.k12.ca.us/lmc/ohs/main/lmc.htm>
The Paidea School Library in Atlanta, Georgia
          <http://www.paideiaschool.org/library/default.htm>
National Cathedral School Libraries in Mt. St. Alban's, Washington, D.C.
          <http://ncs.cathedral.org/uslibrary/Library/amainpage/upperlowerlib.htm>
St. Joseph's Nudgee College Library in Queensland, Australia
          <http://www.nudgee.com/library/>
Rusk High School Library in Rusk, Texas
          <http://www.rusk.esc7.net/rhs/RuskHighSchoolLibrary.htm>
The Lovett School Libraries in Atlanta, Georgia
          <http://www.lovett.org/libraryweb/library.htm>
Washington Township High School in Sewell, New Jersey
          <http://www.wtps.org/wths/imc/index.html>
Chico High School in Chico, California
          <http://dewey.chs.chico.k12.ca.us/>
Edna M. Fielder Elementary School in Katy, Texas
          <http://www.katy.isd.tenet.edu/fe/library/fielderlibrary/fielderlibrary.html>

Internet Sites for Home Page Design and Development

Carnegie Library of Pittsburgh
This site helps librarians develop home pages, provides links to other Web sites, offers free clip art, and discusses various issues dealing with Web design and maintenance. <http://www.clpgh.org/clp/Libraries/webdev.html>

Writing for the Web
This is a general introduction to Web content creation and deals with the concepts and terminology associated with writing or creating documents and resources for a home page.
<http://bones.med.ohio-state.edu/eric/papers/primer/webdocs.html>

Solutions for Site Builders
This site gives information and tips on FrontPage and Dreamweaver as well as domain names.
<http://builder.cnet.com/>

The U.S. Census Bureau
This is a source for demographic information, which is very useful when you design the content of your home page.
<http://www.census.gov/>

Accessible Web Page Design Resources
Check the following sites for Section 508 Guidelines, which are federal government standards for designing home pages that accommodate people with disabilities.
<http://library.uwsp.edu/aschmetz/Accessible/pub_resources.htm>

Bobby
<http://www.cast.org/bobby>

A List Apart
<http://www.alistapart.com/stories/indexAccessibility.html>

Section 508 Home Page
<http://www.section508.gov>

Techniques and Tools for Web Accessibility
<http://www.csusm.edu/accessibility/>

World Wide Web Consortium's Web Accessibility Initiative
<http://www.w3c.org/WAI>

If all this seems like too much work, you can always hire a professional Web designer; many advertise their services on the Internet. There are advantages and disadvantages to hiring a Web designer. If you do not want to create a home page, hiring a designer frees time for you to spend on other projects. On the other hand, with a designer you do not "have a say" in the design, nor the capacity or freedom to make changes and update your home page whenever it is necessary.

Design Considerations

Regardless of whether you design your own home page or have one designed for you, remember to follow basic design techniques.

- A home page ought to be eye-catching, but not hurtful on the eyes; therefore, muted colors are better than harsh, bright colors.
- Graphics, backgrounds, colors, and images should not dominate your home page, but rather enhance it.
- Remember when using graphics and images that smaller files will load faster than larger ones. This is an important factor since most people do not have high-speed modems or cable connections and a page that takes too long to load will dissuade many users from exploring your page.
- Save image files as a .jpeg or .gif with a resolution of 72 pixels per inch. This resolution will keep the image from looking fuzzy.
- A uniform layout is easier to read and navigate, so use the same color scheme and format throughout your home page.
- A good home page has the capability for its users to communicate with you via e-mail. This e-mail interaction also enables one to take advantage of instantaneous communication with experts and professionals in different fields. If nothing else, think of all the trees that are saved by using electronic rather than snail mail!

We have repeated many of the design instructions in each section under design considerations. Although they may seem redundant, they are necessary to make the instructions specific to each type of page.

If you are going to post surveys or forms, you do not have to make up your own. Many of these forms are available with your Web-authoring software, as well as on the Internet. They can be accessed at the following sites and are ready to post on your home page.

Electronic Data Collection
<http://www.forms.com/>
Infopoll
< http://www.accesscable.net/~infopoll/Library.htm>
Forms
<http://www.wiscforms.com/>
Internet Legal Resource Guide
<http://www.ilrg.com/forms/>

Finally, before posting any content to your home page, preview it in commonly used browsers (Internet Explorer and Netscape Navigator) so you can view it online to make sure it loads without any errors before visitors access it. Post your home page only when it is ready; an "under construction" sign does not convey a professional image. We check our links once a month for any broken links that need to be updated or deleted. Sites on the Internet are ephemeral, so in order to remain credible, update constantly.

Copyright Issues

There is a temptation to use any material found on the Internet without giving credit or citing sources. Though there are sites that are public domain and offer free clip art and other material, it is best to be aware of copyright issues. Many of the examples in this book are links to school library home pages. In most instances, these are free of copyright restrictions. According to ALA copyright specialist Carrie Russell, copying URLs from another home page to yours is permissible. However, permission is suggested if you want to link your home page to one that belongs to someone else. The following Web sites offer extensive information on this subject.

Copyright and Fair Use Information
           <http://fairuse.stanford.edu>
United States Patent and Trademark Office
           <http://www.uspto.gov>
Copyright Web Site
           <http://www.benedict.com/>
NOLO, a site that offers self-help legal information.
           <http://www.nolo.com>

When in doubt, it is always better to err on the side of caution and ask for permission to use the site!

Promoting Your Home Page

Educators are aware of the link between academic achievement and libraries. Students who attend schools with well-funded libraries achieve higher reading test scores than those who don't. Providing and publicizing everything that your library does to implement the school library's central mission and to support the school's academic goals could result in fiscal support for your library and its programs.

After you build your home page, you will need maximum exposure. If no one can find your home page, it does not matter how informative and useful it is. Here are some ways to ensure that your home page will get maximum exposure.

Promote your home page by distributing your URL not only to various search engines and subject indexes, but also to the media, advertisements via newsletters, and word of mouth. All letterheads and business cards should carry your URL. All of your home page promotional needs can be found at the following site:

Web Site Promotional Center
           <http://www.submit-away.com/>

Include your e-mail address on your home page to enable users to provide feedback on your page and inform you if some of the links are not functioning. This allows you to keep your home page current.

Go to Web pages that relate to your subject. E-mail the authors of those sites with a description of your page and ask to exchange links so that you are linked to each other's pages.

Impress people who visit your home page by responding quickly to their queries. This timely response will provide a personal touch to their research and visitors will be impressed to discover that they can count on reliable, efficient, and prompt responses from you. This will make it more likely that they will return to your home page.

Post short lists of newsgroups that deal with your subject. Keep your pages and links current so visitors will appreciate the reliability of your information and return for new updates.

Encourage visitors to return to your page by inviting them to bookmark it. When a page is bookmarked, its address is saved on the browser so just a click on the browser's bookmark will return the visitor to the site.

Post any awards or complimentary feedback that your home page receives.

Finally, if a picture is worth a thousand words, a home page will have even more of an impact. By building and promoting a home page, you will be in the public's eye all year instead of just during National Library Week.

Chapter Two

2

Teacher Outreach

Introduction

The library is the center of the school's integrated curriculum, a hub of activity, where students are actively engaged in learning. A library program is developed through collaboration with teachers in designing programs that create a learning community. However, this collaboration does not happen by itself; it requires a well-planned promotional campaign that is focused toward teachers and their curriculum needs. Teacher "word of mouth" is one of the best forms of advertising that can result in the library becoming the first place for teacher planning, activities, resources, and professional development.

Traditional promotional methods included both informal contacts, such as meeting teachers in hallways and lunchrooms, and more formal contacts through flyers, brochures, and newsletters. Previously, these methods were hit or miss. It was common for the library's promotional material to be misplaced, thrown in the trash, or read after the material became outdated. Use of a home page offers a new approach to building partnerships with teachers and promoting the library program.

The following are examples of services that can be provided to teachers via your home page that will promote your library program.

Teacher Assignment Page

A teacher assignment page is the electronic version of a pathfinder for research projects. The teacher's assignment is posted to the library home page with links to the assignment, due dates, and resources such as books, online databases, Web sites, and magazines. It is a means of extending the collaborative process and promoting your library.

Planning the Teacher Assignment Page

First, meet with the teacher to discuss the research project and the areas of responsibility. This can be done during a formal meeting or informally through e-mail. The responsibility for the teacher assignment page is shared. The teacher creates a handout for the research project that includes a description of the assignment, due dates, requirements, a scoring rubric, and evaluation. This handout is saved as an .HTML file so it can be easily inserted into the teacher assignment section of the library's home page. This simple step will save you time because you will not have to redo the research project handout.

Then the media specialist locates the resources, both print and electronic, for the electronic pathfinder and posts these to the teacher assignment page. Finally, the media specialist and the teacher introduce the research project to the students in the library. The teacher assignment page is displayed using an LCD projector and screen, and the teacher explains the assignment while the media specialist introduces the resources that the students will use for their research. Introducing the assignment in the library and using the teacher assignment page as a visual for the lesson reinforces the importance of the library's home page as an instructional tool.

Design Considerations for the Teacher Assignment Page

The teacher assignment page can be organized as an alphabetical list or table using the teacher's name as the link to the research project's name. Thus, more than one assignment can be posted under the teacher's name. For example, Mr. History can have assignments for Imperialism and The Great Depression.

Post a description of the assignment, due dates, requirements, and rubric under each research project. Next, post links to print and electronic resources. Electronic resources include links to online databases and Internet sites. Annotate all Internet sites so the students know the content of each site.

Include navigational links to direct students to the teacher assignment page from the home page. Be sure to maintain a consistent format. The teacher assignment page should use the same colors, graphics, and fonts as the rest of the home page.

Once you have created the page, you can easily update the research projects and pathfinders. Just change the due dates and correct any broken links.

Examples of Teacher Assignment Pages

Washington Township High School IMC in Sewell, New Jersey
<http://wtps.org/wths/imc/assign.htm>
Groves Media Center in Birmingham, Michigan
<http://www.birmingham.k12.mi.us/gro-mc1/>
Lincoln-Way Media Center in Chicago, Illinois
<http://www.lwhs.will.k12.il.us/Library/assignments.htm>

Promoting the Teacher Assignment Page

Initially, this service is advertised at a faculty meeting and then followed up through e-mail to the teachers. Encourage teachers to use this service by e-mailing examples of what other teachers in their department have posted to the library's home page.

These electronic pathfinders will have teachers banging at your door and will generate publicity for your program as teachers tell students and parents about this resource. For instance, teachers will refer their students to their pathfinders during class, while parents are given the library home page address at back-to-school night and told to look at the teacher assignment page for their children's assignments. Now the page is being promoted to teachers, parents, and students—talk about visibility for your program!

Reservation Calendar

Teachers spend many hours in the evening planning their lessons. Frequently they will develop a research assignment without knowing if the library is available for their classes on the days they have planned to present the assignment. Your home page is the solution for this dilemma. Post a monthly reservation calendar that shows the dates and times when classes are scheduled to use the library. This service will assist teachers in planning their lessons and will generate goodwill for your program because it makes using the library convenient for them. The reservation calendar is also another way for you to promote your program with the administration. At the end of each month, e-mail the address of the calendar to the principal, so he or she can see the number of classes that used the library. This will highlight the library's instructional role in the curriculum.

Planning the Reservation Calendar

In order for the calendar to be useful to teachers, it is crucial that you maintain it on a daily basis. Updating the calendar should take no longer than 10 minutes each day. There are three notices to include with the calendar. First, inform the teachers about the number of classes that can be accommodated per period. Second, include a disclaimer stating that the calendar is subject to change based on availability. Third, you definitely want your teachers to know they must call or e-mail you to schedule their classes. This allows you to discuss the assignment with them and extend the collaborative process.

Design Considerations for the Reservation Calendar

The link for the reservation calendar is located on your teacher assignment page or your professional development page. On the first page of the calendar include its purpose and any disclaimers. Then organize the dates and times available into a list arranged by weeks. Be sure to post the calendar for a minimum of four weeks. This provides your teachers with enough time to schedule their classes. Next, use a table format to display the dates and times that are available each week. If a class has reserved the library, include the teacher's name on the date and time. Finally, include your e-mail address on the page (see Figure 2.1).

Examples of Reservation Calendars
Coral Gables Media Center in Coral Gables, Florida
<http://cghs.dadeschools.net/library/calendar/reservations.htm>
California Middle School Library Media Center in Long Beach, California
<http://www.calendars.net:8189/califmslmccal>
Mullen Hall Library Media Center in Falmouth, Massachusetts
<http://www.falmouth.k12.ma.us/mh/schedule.html>

Promoting the Reservation Calendar

The best way to advertise this service is to e-mail teachers to notify them that the home page can be used to check the availability of the library for their classes. Be sure to include

Figure 2.1   Library Reservation Calendar

Happy High School Library
Class Schedule

This calendar shows the dates that the library is available for your classes. The library can accommodate up to two classes per period. Please be aware that this calendar is updated on a daily basis and availability is subject to change.

Please contact the library by e-mail or by calling ext. 21.

Weekly Calendar

9/3-9/6   9/10-9/14   9/17-9/21   9/24-9/28

Periods	Monday	Tuesday	Wednesday	Thursday	Friday
			Week of September 3–6		
1	Hudson Monroe	Hudson	Hudson		
2		Smith	Smith		Jones
3				Cullen	Cullen
4					
5					
6					
7	Jones				

SUBMIT   CLEAR

the address of the home page in the e-mail. You can also publicize this service during faculty meetings and in your library's newsletter. The teachers will appreciate the convenience of this service and it is another opportunity to promote your library's program.

Professional Development

Traditionally, a section or room in the library is reserved for professional development materials, where teachers access information about current trends in their profession. Today, the professional development center can be part of your home page and the hub for professional development opportunities. This translates into more visibility for your library program.

Professional development is a helpful service for your library to offer teachers as it allows them to stay on the cutting edge of their profession. This is especially important, since more and more states are mandating continuing education for teachers. It is also a natural extension of the collaborative process; it allows you to provide opportunities for teachers to gain knowledge and develop expertise to enhance student learning.

Planning Professional Development Workshops

Contact your administration and inform them that as part of the district's long-term professional development plan, you would like to design and teach Web-based workshops to assist teachers in integrating technology into the curriculum. These workshops will be scheduled as part of the district's inservice program with workshop materials and handouts posted on your home page. Before implementing these workshops, you will have to do several things. Post all instructions and deadlines for registration. Delineate the levels of computer skills needed to complete the course. Next, provide ongoing support for teachers to successfully complete the Web-based workshops. Teachers should have the opportunity to ask questions and voice concerns regarding the content of the workshop. E-mail is an excellent way to answer their questions. Let teachers know that you check your e-mail at certain times during the day and will get back to them immediately. In fact, provide a link to your e-mail with the times that you are available on the workshop agenda page. Also, if you cannot resolve their questions with e-mail, set up a time to personally meet with them. Sometimes all that is needed is a quick demonstration to resolve a problem. Finally, award professional development credits for the workshops. Evidence of completing the workshop could be a project they use in their classrooms to enhance the learning environment for their students.

To accurately determine the technology needs of your teachers, conduct surveys and informal interviews (see Figure 2.2). Distribute the surveys using e-mail or by placing them in the teachers' mailboxes at the beginning of the school year.

Content of the Workshops

Teachers want practical staff development opportunities they can immediately use in their classrooms and are particularly interested in hands-on projects that will help them infuse technology into their curriculum. Your library's home page can become a virtual professional development center by offering workshops that teachers can use to enhance their knowledge and hone their technology skills. The content of these online workshops should be geared to what teachers need to integrate technology into their lessons and can include Web Searching, PowerPoint and Web Page Design—the possibilities are limitless.

Figure 2.2 Technology Survey

Happy High School
Library's Technology Survey

Dear Teachers,

The library will be conducting technology workshops during the school year and would like your help in determining the type of workshops that would help you with integrating technology into the curriculum.

I use search strategies to locate information on the Internet
   ◎ Not at all   ◎ Somewhat   ◎ Very well

I know how to locate information on online databases
   ◎ Not at all   ◎ Somewhat   ◎ Very well

I use word processing software (Word, Works, WordPerfect)
   ◎ Not at all   ◎ Somewhat   ◎ Very well

I use a Web-authoring program (such as FrontPage or Composer) to design Web pages
   ◎ Not at all   ◎ Somewhat   ◎ Very well

I use e-mail
   ◎ Not at all   ◎ Somewhat   ◎ Very well

I use databases (Access)
   ◎ Not at all   ◎ Somewhat   ◎ Very well

I use spreadsheets (Excel)
   ◎ Not at all   ◎ Somewhat   ◎ Very well

I use presentation programs (such as HyperStudio or PowerPoint)
   ◎ Not at all   ◎ Somewhat   ◎ Very well

I know how to use
    video cameras   ◎ Not at all   ◎ Somewhat   ◎ Very well
    digital cameras   ◎ Not at all   ◎ Somewhat   ◎ Very well
    scanners   ◎ Not at all   ◎ Somewhat   ◎ Very well

Describe how you use technology in your classroom.

SUBMIT   CLEAR

Start with your area of expertise. If you are the guru of Internet searching, start there because the first time designing a workshop is always the most difficult. Keep in mind that designing a workshop is time consuming; you should allow two to three months from planning to presentation. Once you have the workshop completed and posted to your home page, it can be used over and over again with minor revisions.

Organize your workshops as how-to manuals with links to resources. Review Web-based workshops that media specialists have posted to their home pages. These can serve as models for your workshops. In particular, look at the organizational structure, content, and format.

Examples of Professional Development Workshops Designed and Presented by Media Specialists

Web Development
Joyce Valenza of Springfield High School in Pennsylvania teaches a variety of technology workshops on her library's links; one of these workshops can be found at
<http://mciunix.mciu.k12.pa.us/~spjvweb/webquests.html>

Teaching with Primary Sources
Debbie Abilock, the librarian at Nueva High School in Hillsborough, California, created this online course.
<http://nuevaschool.org/~debbie/library/outreach/cnd.html>

Internet Basics for Educators
Linda Bertland, the librarian at Stetson Middle School in Philadelphia, Pennsylvania, created this helpful course.
<http://www.sldirectory.com/compf/iclass.html#top>

Search the Web Webquest
This staff development workshop is one of many created by Rob Darrow, the librarian at Alta Sierra Intermediate School in Clovis, California.
<http://www.clovisusd.k12.ca.us/alta/lmc/searchquest2.html>

After reviewing these workshops and examining the results of your survey, determine your own goals and objectives; these should be practical and focused. For example, after attending the Internet workshop, you will use search strategies to locate information in your subject area. You can even align these to your state or national standards. Delineate the prerequisite computer skills; you don't want teachers who are novice technology users to become frustrated. It is a good idea to offer two levels of workshops, one for novices and one for advanced users.

Next, set the agenda for the workshop. The agenda should include the topics covered during the workshop and a schedule for the day's activities (see Figure 2.3). Be sure to include time for breaks and for independent practice. If it is a full-day workshop, use the morning for instruction and the afternoon for practice.

Design Considerations for Professional Development Workshops

The same design rules that you use for your library's home page apply to the professional development page. Maintain a consistent format using the same font size, colors, and graphics. Always include navigational tools, so your teachers can easily return to the various sections of the workshop and the index of the home page.

Create a new link on the index page of your library's home page entitled professional development. Organize your workshop titles as a list or a table. Then create a link from each workshop to the table of contents. For example, the table of contents might include a description of the workshop, goals and objectives, the agenda, and a list of topics. Each topic should include a brief explanation and links to resources. Finally, use an online form so participants can evaluate the workshop (see Figure 2.4). Don't worry about learning how to create forms because most Web-authoring programs include form makers and there are many sites on the Internet to obtain free form makers. One site is FormSite.com; all you have to do is register.

Promoting Professional Development Workshops and Courses

Advertise workshops in your district's staff development brochures, at faculty meetings, on your library's home page, and through e-mail. After a few teachers have successfully completed these courses, word of mouth will be your best advertisement and will promote your library as a technology leader.

Professional Development Collection

The Internet is like a giant bookstore where everything available is not necessarily the best. Teachers lead hectic lives and usually do not have time to find the best sites for lesson plans, collaborative projects, or educational topics of interest. Therefore, you can provide a much-needed service by locating and posting sites to your home page that are based on accuracy, objectivity, currency, and authority. This service enables teachers to turn to the library's home page because they know it has the best sites to offer. It simplifies research for teachers and enhances their professional development opportunities, while at the same time promoting the library as a technology leader.

As part of collection development, locate exemplary sites in professional journals, on other librarians' home pages, and on education portals. E-mail your teachers to see if they have sites they would like to add to the collection.

Design Considerations for the Professional Development Collection

Once you have located sites that support your professional development collection, create a category called teacher sites, and post it under the professional development page of your library's home page. Organize these links into a user-friendly format such as a list or table with headings that indicate the content; for example, lesson plans, subject sites, collaborative projects, and professional organizations.

All sites should connect directly to the information and not to links of links; annotate with clear, concise descriptions of the content. Again, adhere to the guidelines used to set up your home page and keep the same format, colors, and graphics. Also, navigation tools should be consistent and should return the user to the index of your home page.

Figure 2.3 Workshop Template

Happy High School
Technology Workshop

Description of the Workshop

This workshop will explain

Prerequisite Technology Skills

Objectives

You will be able to

1.

2.

3.

Schedule of Activities

Evaluation

SUBMIT   CLEAR

Figure 2.4 Workshop Evaluation Form

Workshop Evaluation Form

Please rate the workshop

On the whole, the workshop met its objective.

   ◎ Excellent ◎ Good ◎ Fair ◎ Poor

The instructor was well prepared and organized.

   ◎ Excellent ◎ Good ◎ Fair ◎ Poor

The instructor assisted students on an individual basis.

   ◎ Excellent ◎ Good ◎ Fair ◎ Poor

The workshop was appropriate to my computer skill level.

   ◎ Excellent ◎ Good ◎ Fair ◎ Poor

There was a balance between instruction and time for practice.

   ◎ Excellent ◎ Good ◎ Fair ◎ Poor

Check Yes or No for the following:

I would recommend this workshop to other teachers.

   ◎ Yes ◎ No

I will use what I learned from this workshop.

   ◎ Yes ◎ No

The instructor should spend more time on

The instructor should spend less time on

I learned the following

SUBMIT   CLEAR

Technology FAQs

Many teachers are embarrassed to admit they are not computer savvy, but sometimes all they need is a quick refresher or more information about the Internet or a software program. Your home page can become a virtual help desk for frequently asked questions (FAQs) about technology. These technology tips can include saving pictures, search strategies, copying a URL into e-mail, or using word art. The FAQs will be as varied as the questions teachers ask.

Develop the Technology FAQs section of your home page by designing your own technology tips or linking to help files already on the Web.

Design Considerations for Technology FAQs

When designing your own technology tips, start with software programs that are the most frequently used and generate the most questions. These technology tips should be no longer than one or two pages and should provide step-by-step directions. Be sure to include pictures with the explanations because a picture provides more information and is easier to understand.

If you are going to create links to help files on the Web, be sure to connect directly to the technology tips and not to a list of links. You don't want to waste your teachers' time.

The following are sites that provide technology tips:
Microsoft Products
                <http://support.microsoft.com/directory/faqs.asp?sd=gn&fr=0>
Netscape
                <http://home.netscape.com/browsers/6/faq.html?cp=n6ilnvfaq>
Hyperstudio
                <http://www.hyperstudio.com/faqs/index.html#technical>
ClarisWorks
                <http://www.apple.com/education/k12/products/appleworks/tips/>
Adobe Acrobat Reader
                <http://www.adobe.com/support/techguides/acrobat/main.html>
Scanning
                <http://www.scantips.com>

Under the professional development page on your library's home page, post a new link entitled FAQs. Remember to keep the format and navigation tools consistent with other sections of the home page.

Examples of Technology FAQs

Selah Middle School Library in Selah, Washington
                <http://share3.esd105.wednet.edu/mccayb/UsingNewTechnology.htm>
Park City High School Library in Park City, Utah
                <http://www.parkcity.k12.ut.us/LibraryWebSite/default.html>

Promoting Technology FAQs

The visibility of your library will increase as you direct teachers to the FAQs section of your home page when they e-mail or stop by the library for technology help.

Virtual Faculty Room

A faculty room is one of the best places for teachers to informally share ideas and experiences as it helps them stay connected to each other and keep up with what is going on educationally in their school. In comparison, the Internet is a global faculty room as it brings together educators from all over the world through discussion groups, listservs, and chat rooms. There are numerous advantages to creating a virtual faculty room. It allows teachers to communicate with each other when it is convenient for them. It broadens their educational perspective because it includes educators on all levels from various countries and from many subject disciplines.

Design Considerations for the Virtual Faculty Room

You don't have to develop your own listserv to design a virtual faculty room. Create a link called virtual faculty room on the professional development page of your library's home page and post the Web sites of education discussion groups, listservs, and chat rooms. It should take no longer than a day or two to post this new service to your home page. Also, it will be helpful to your teachers if you include an explanation of the purpose of the virtual faculty room. This explanation should remind your teachers that these discussions or chats are free, but they will have to complete a registration form.

The following are Web sites that you might want to include on your virtual faculty room.

Teacher Talk Chat Room
> <http://www.learninghow.com/teachertalk.html>

Teacher Talk Forums
> <http://www.teaching.com/ttalk/>

After School Online
> <http://www.tappedin.org/>

Chalk Talk Online
> <http://www.chalktalkonline.com/>

Teachers Net
> <http://teachers.net/chat/>

Examples of Virtual Faculty Rooms

Hompkinton High School Library in Contoocook, New Hampshire
> <http://www.hopkinton.k12.nh.us/groups/hhslibrary/teachersroom.html>

Byron Middle School Library in Byron, Illinois
> <http://www.leeogle.org/byron/bms/tpp.htm>

Bedford Middle School Library in Westport, Connecticut
> <http://bms.westport.k12.ct.us/lmc/teachersrm.htm>

Promoting the Virtual Faculty Room

Talk up this new service at faculty and department meetings, in your newsletters, and through e-mail. Offer mini-workshops during and after school to show teachers how to register and use chat rooms and listservs. This service promotes the library and its involvement in your teachers' professional development.

New Teachers

New teachers in your school, though very excited about their jobs, can be easily over-whelmed with all of the things they must learn in a short period of time. Here is an excellent opportunity to provide a service to these new teachers and show them that the library is their first stop for information and service.

Schedule an orientation to the library as part of the new teacher orientation pro-gram. New teachers are eager to learn what you can do to help them and this is a golden opportunity to showcase your library and its many programs. After the teachers have completed a physical tour of the library, they will take a virtual tour via your home page. Direct them to the teacher assignment page and the professional development page including tutorials, workshops, and links. Point out that new arrivals are always posted to the home page and they should frequently check the home page for the latest updates. Then, show them the virtual faculty room where they can join listservs and discussion groups and meet educators from all over the world.

Create a link on your home page specifically designed for new teachers where bell schedules, testing days, the monthly school calendar, notices for the end of the mark-ing period, articles on classroom management, and hints for new teachers are posted.

Design Considerations for the New Teacher Page

Make it easy for your new teachers to locate the new teacher page by placing this cate-gory on the index page of your library's home page. Be sure to keep the design format and navigation tools consistent with the other pages.

If you are going to post bell schedules, the monthly school calendars, and teach-ers' handbook, don't reinvent the wheel; this information is available in a text format. Just ask your administration to e-mail you this information. All you will have to do is cut and paste this into your Web-authoring program. It will save you hours of work.

There are many excellent Internet sites that provide support to new teachers. Here are a few that you might want to include on your new teacher page.

TeachNet: New Teachers Online
<http://www.teachnet.org/mtol>
ADPRIMA
<http://www.adprima.com>
Survival Kit for New Teachers
<http://www.inspiringteachers.com>
Survival Guide for New Teachers
<http://www.ed.gov/pubs/survivalguide/>
Master Teacher Discipline Guides
<http://www.disciplinehelp.com/home.cfm>

Example of a New Teacher Page

Desert Sky Middle School Library in Glendale, Arizona
<http://desertsky.dvusd.org/LMC/dsms_lmc_index.html>

Promoting the New Teacher Page

You can showcase the new teacher page as well as your library program at the new teacher orientation. Follow up the orientation by e-mailing new teachers notices of updates to the new teacher page throughout the year. This will continue to promote your library as a place that cares about new teachers and provides services to make them successful.

New Materials

Teachers love it when new books, videos, or CDs arrive in the library. Your library's home page is an excellent tool to notify your staff. Instead of printing out lists and putting them in teachers' mailboxes, e-mail the address for the new materials section of your home page to them. This is a quick and easy service that promotes your library.

Design Considerations for the New Materials Page

Create a new category called new materials on the index page of the library's home page. This is an ideal section for using graphics. Organize each section for books, videos, and CDs into lists using a graphic as the link. For example, you can use graphics such as a book, CD, or videocassette. Keep the size of the image small and use .jpegs and .gifs for your graphic files. In addition, don't forget to include text descriptions with the images for people with disabilities. Date the page so teachers will know that the list is current.

Once you set up the lists for new materials, it is very easy to maintain. All you have to do is delete the data under each heading and update it with the new arrivals. This is a time saver because you no longer have to put the new material lists in teachers' mailboxes.

Examples of New Materials Pages

Caribou High School Media Center in Caribou, Maine
<http://www.caribou.k12.me.us/secondary/chs/library/library.html>
Amsterdam High School Media Center in New Amsterdam, New York
<http://www.gasd.org/highschool/media/newarrivals.htm>
St. Mary Magdalen Library Media Center in Wilmington, Delaware
<http://www.stmary.pvt.k12.de.us/Library.html#New Arrivals>

Promoting the New Materials Page

Each time you post new books, videos, or CDs, e-mail the teachers and let them know that they can browse the new arrivals by going to the library's home page. Be sure to include your library's address in the e-mail. Teachers will appreciate this service and it will generate publicity for your program.

Chapter Three

Service to Students

Introduction

The most rewarding aspect of our jobs as media specialists is working with students. There is nothing more satisfying than the look of appreciation after you have helped a student with a research question. Now the Internet is transforming our vision of the library and the type of service that we can provide to our students. We have the capability through a home page to provide around-the-clock service to our students and to become an electronic community and learning center. Here students can visit an online reference center, ask a librarian for homework help, post an electronic book review, publish an online magazine, access an online catalog and databases, or chat with friends. The possibilities of service to students are limitless. A home page is the key to providing service and information in a new way to students and creating a virtual community of learners who are library lovers.

Here are some ways to hook your students into becoming bibliophiles and promote your library program at the same time.

Student Advisory Board

One way to actively involve students in your library is to create a student advisory board where students assist in program planning, reader's advisory, marketing, and Web page design.

Recruiting Members
There are several ways to involve students in your advisory board. Invite your regular library users to join the board. E-mail your teachers and have them nominate students to serve on the board. Finally, use the school's daily announcements to recruit new members.

Organizing the Student Advisory Board

At the first meeting, the members determine the following things: the purpose of the student advisory board, meeting dates and times, and activities. At first, the students probably won't know what type of activities to plan, so give them a list of suggested activities. Include planning programs such as story time, selecting new books, CDs and videos, or creating displays or videos about the library. A very meaningful and engaging activity for the student advisory board is the creation of home pages for their peers. Next, organize committees according to the activities that the students select for the year. For example, students who are interested in Web page design would join the Web committee while students interested in reading would volunteer for story time or reader's advisory.

Student Advisory Board Teen Page

Students naturally gravitate to the Internet and a way to tap into their enthusiasm is to have your student advisory board design a home page for teens. This project will benefit the students and the library's program. The creation of a home page allows the students to work as a team, learn new technologies, and contribute positively to their school. In turn, this will generate publicity for the library as students look for the teen page on your home page.

Planning the Teen Page

This is a student activity; they are responsible for the design, content, and maintenance of the home page. This activity will be very time consuming in the beginning for you, the advisor, as you work with the students to organize and plan the home pages. One of the first things to do is review the district's Web publishing policy with the students so they will know the district's guidelines for publishing their work on the Web. Discuss the criteria to use in selecting sites for the teen page. As the advisor, you are responsible for the content of the Web pages, so review the sites that students have selected; this can be done as part of your student advisory board meeting.

If no one on the advisory board knows .HTML or a Web-authoring program, you can teach a few students the fundamentals of a Web-authoring program and have them train the other board members. If you teach a few students from each grade level, you won't have to retrain the students each year. If this is too time consuming, work with your school's computer club. The computer club can post and maintain the site while the student advisory board can design the teen page and select the sites. It is critical that once the Web page is posted that links remain current. This is a time-consuming task that can be made easier, if the students share the maintenance of the Web page. The best way to do this is to assign students from your advisory board to serve as editors and assume responsibility for maintaining a section of the teen page. Also, post an e-mail address so users can notify the Webmaster if they find a broken link.

One of the first things that the students should do is select a name for the teen page. The name should direct other students to this link on the library's home page. Some suggested names based on the age of the students are Teen Zone, For Teens Only, Kids' Stuff, and Teen Cyber Room.

The students might also want a logo for their page. The design of the logo presents a wider opportunity to involve other students in the teen page. The student advisory board could sponsor a logo contest open to all students in the school. Advertise this contest on the library's home page, in the school's daily announcements, and e-mail notices to teachers.

Content of the Teen Page

The content will be as varied as the students on the advisory board and should reflect the interests of the students in the school. Include an e-mail link on the page so students can suggest sites to the student advisory board.

Content can include links to college information, horoscopes, and entertainment sites including sports, music, movies, games, and television shows. The content should also be interactive, allowing teens to submit reviews of books, movies, music, and television shows. Collaborate with your language arts teachers and have their students submit reviews as part of a writing activity.

Links to chat and e-mail can foster this interactivity; make sure this is permissible under your district's safety standards policies. Another feature to include on the home page is a local teen help line. The help line lists places in the community to get help for personal problems and include links to drug and alcohol agencies, personal counseling, and suicide prevention.

Focus attention on the student advisory board by including pictures of the advisory board, activities, meeting dates, and membership requirements. Be sure to follow district guidelines regarding publishing students' names and pictures and obtain any release forms that are required.

Design Considerations for the Teen Page

The teen page will reflect the students' creativity and will use graphics, banners, backgrounds, bright colors, and varying font styles. Graphics should be age appropriate. Keep files sizes small and use a .gif or .jpeg format, otherwise the page will take too long to load.

Make the link for the teen page a category on the index of the library's home page. The content can be organized into frames, tables, or lists and should include navigational tools directing the users to the index of the home page.

Examples of Teen Pages

Conard High School Media Center in West Hartford, Connecticut
           <http://www.whps.org/School/CONARD/index.asp>
BRHS Library Media Center in Boothbay Harbor, Maine
           <http://home.gwi.net/brhs/new.html>

Promoting the Teen Page

This is an instance where "word of mouth" is your best advertisement. Students enjoy showing off their accomplishments and they will tell their parents, relatives, teachers, administrators, and friends about the teen page. Each visit to your home page is an advertisement for your library program that creates visibility in the school and in the community.

E-zines

Teachers are always looking for class projects that engage their students in authentic learning, while students want to share their talent and creativity, not only with their peers, but also with a wider audience beyond the school walls. Publishing an online magazine, or e-zine, is an activity that can make that happen. An e-zine is a collaborative activity that will generate enthusiasm among students and teachers. You couldn't buy a better advertisement for your library's program than an e-zine on your home page. It will definitely create a high-profile presence for your library as students, parents, teachers, and administrators discover the benefits of publishing on the Web.

Planning an E-zine

Creating an electronic magazine, or e-zine, is a project that is both collaborative and interdisciplinary and involves the language arts department, the art department, the business or technology department, and the library. At the elementary level this collaboration could involve the entire school. Initially, there should not be more than one teacher from each department involved in creating the online magazine. Work with one grade level. Start small, and only publish one or two issues the first year because organizing and piloting the first e-zine involves a great deal of coordination, planning, and time. Since the e-zine is a collaborative project, delineating the areas of responsibilities is the first task to accomplish. The media specialist is the liaison among the departments, coordinates the activity, and instructs the students on accessing and evaluating information. The language arts teacher is responsible for the content of the e-zine, while students determine the theme for each issue and write and edit all submissions. The art teacher is responsible for the submission of student artwork to illustrate the e-zine. The business or technology teacher's students use a Web-authoring program to design the layout for the online magazine.

The second task is scheduling meetings to organize the e-zine. Initially, these meetings should be formally scheduled, but once the e-zine is organized, use e-mail to communicate with each other. Finally, set up a publication schedule; this schedule should include all deadlines so the teachers can design their lesson plans for the activity.

Content of the E-zine

The e-zine is student oriented and includes original essays, stories, poems, interviews, reviews of books, movies, music, and television shows. Student artwork should be original and coordinate with the text. Have a theme for each issue. Also, include the names of the contributors, along with the names of the teachers and classes, who published the e-zine. Don't forget to check your district's policy regarding the publication of students' names.

Design Considerations for the E-zine

When first organizing your e-zine, use a storyboarding technique with 3- x 5-inch cards representing Web pages. This will enable the students to visualize the layout of the e-zine with all of its links. Make one card the index of the e-zine and then arrange the other cards in the order that the students want them linked on the page. They can rearrange the cards before actually creating the e-zine.

Since this is an online magazine, the first page includes the name of the e-zine and the publication date; it should be beautifully designed with a graphic that illustrates the theme of the issue. Include a logo, if you think the e-zine needs a visual representation. The fonts, colors, and background should allow for student self-expression and creativity. Carefully edit each article for content, spelling, and grammar because the e-zine will be available to a worldwide audience.

The e-zine's interface should be user friendly and consistent from issue to issue. The best interface to use with an e-zine is a frames format because the index and content are both visible at the same time on the computer screen. The frames format also allows for ease of navigation. Use two vertical frames, one for the index and one for the table of contents. The index frame is the smaller of the two and is placed on the left side. The index frame is the table of contents of the current issue and includes links to back issues (see Figure 3.1).

Figure 3.1 Sample Frames Format

Name of E-zine	**Name of the E-zine**
Table of Contents	**Publication Date** **Theme**
Contributors	
Back Issues **Spring** **Winter**	**Graphic/Image Illustrates the Theme**

All artwork is scanned or created digitally and saved as a .jpeg or .gif file format and all text submissions are submitted by e-mail or on a disk and saved as .HTML. This makes it easier for the students designing the layout to cut and paste the text into the e-zine.

Promoting the E-zine

The students and teachers who published the e-zine are going to "talk up" their accomplishment to teachers, students, the administration, and their families. Every time someone accesses the e-zine, your library's home page and its services are showcased.

Reference and Homework Help

The amount of information on the Internet is overwhelming and searching the Web can be a daunting task. Yet, students will ignore all other information sources and randomly search the Web for information that may not be very reliable. Additionally, students lead overscheduled lives, which often do not coincide with library hours. As instructional leaders, it is important for us to provide our students with access to information when it is convenient for them and to organize this information so it meets their research needs. Once students realize the library's home page is a treasure trove of information, they will make it their first stop during the research process. Each time students use the reference and homework help section of your home page, it reinforces the positive image of the library in their lives.

Planning Reference and Homework Help

The same criteria that applies to the selection of print resources also applies to the Internet. Sites are selected for their accuracy, authority, currency, and objectivity. You can locate exemplary sites in professional journals, ALA's 700+ Great Sites, other librarians' home pages and education portals. Also, students working on research assignments are a source for excellent sites; ask them to give you the names and URLs of the sites they locate so you can add them to your home page.

Design Considerations for Reference and Homework Help

All sites should connect directly to the information and not to links of links. Annotate all sites with clear, concise descriptions of the content. Adhere to the guidelines used in setting up your home page and keep the same format, colors, and graphics. Also, navigation tools should be consistent and return the user to main menu of the home page.

Once you have located sites that support your school's curriculum, post them to the index page of the library's home page as curriculum links and hotlists.

Curriculum Links

Organize curriculum links into an easy-to-use format and post them to the index page of your home page. There are myriad ways to organize your curriculum links including Dewey numbers, subject headings, categories, image maps, or a combination of these.

Using Dewey numbers for your curriculum links complements the organizational structure of your print collection. The format can be arranged as either a list or table using the 10 main classification numbers. Use a text description for each subdivision of the main classes. For example, the 900s History and Geography would include links to General History, Geography and Travel, and Biography. To see an example of the use of Dewey numbers to organize curriculum links, visit the Minnetonka Middle School West, Minnetonka, MN. <http://www.minnetonka.k12.mn.us/mmw/media/media.html#Dewey%20Decimal%20Web%20Sites>

Subject headings based on your school's curriculum are an easy way to organize your links. The format can be a list or table and arranged alphabetically for ease of use. Subject headings can be further divided according to your school's curriculum. For example, the science links can be divided into astronomy, biology, chemistry, and physical science. To see an example of a school library that uses a subject-heading format, visit the Hatboro Horsham High School Library in Horsham, Pennsylvania. <http://www.hatboro-horsham.org/shs/HH_Library/default.htm>

Curriculum links can also be organized into broad topics or categories, which can be arranged into a table format. For example, categories might include links to encyclopedias, endangered species, health, and Web evaluation. To see an example of a school library that uses categories, visit the North Library at State College High School in State College, Pennsylvania. <http://www.scasd.k12.pa.us/HSLibNo/>

An image map is another way to organize your curriculum links. An image map uses a picture with links that are activated when you click on them. For example, an image map for curriculum links might use a globe for geography, a book for language arts, or a microscope for science. Although an image map might look cute on your home page, it really isn't very practical, especially for people with disabilities. So, if you use an image map, be sure to use text descriptions with each picture. To see an example of a school library that uses an image map, visit the Archbishop Ryan High School Library in Philadelphia, Pennsylvania. <http://www.ryanhs.org/library/>

Hotlists

A hotlist is a collection of frequently used Internet sites on a specific topic. It is similar to the "bookmarks" in Netscape and "my favorites" in Explorer. Hotlists provide an opportunity to integrate information skills into the curriculum, cooperatively plan lessons, and provide quality resources for students.

Planning Hotlists

Hotlists can be prepared by the media specialist or as a collaborative project between the media specialist and teachers. The ideal way to set up hotlists is to collaborate with the subject teacher. It is also an excellent method to integrate information skills into the curriculum. First, meet with the teacher to discuss the topics for the hotlist and the areas of responsibility. The teacher's curriculum determines the content of the hotlists. The content can be for a specific topic or the year's curriculum. Next, the teacher organizes the students into groups of two to search for topics, and the media specialist develops a Web Site Evaluation Form for evaluating the Web sites (see Figure 3.2), and conducts lessons on Web evaluation and search strategies.

The students locate quality Web sites on their topic, thereby assuming responsibility for their own learning. The students complete topic site evaluation forms and turn these in to the media specialist who reviews them with the teacher and selects the sites for the hotlist.

Design Considerations for Hotlists

The media specialist or the teacher compiles the list of sites for each topic. If the teacher compiles the list, it should be saved as an .HTML file so it can be easily inserted into the Web-authoring program that you use. The media specialist creates a hotlist link on the index page of the library's home page. The hotlist page can be formatted as a table and organized by topic, grade, or teacher's name. Include navigation links directing students back to the home page.

Figure 3.2 Web Site Evaluation Form

Names and Period

The Best Sites on the Web

Directions: Working in pairs, you will evaluate Web sites to determine which sites will be included in a hotlist to be used for research in this class during the year. As you evaluate each site, please complete this form.

Topic

Name of the Site

Description of the Site's Content

Evaluation Check List: Circle Yes or No

◉ Yes   ◉ No   Is the author's name on the page?

◉ Yes   ◉ No   Is there a date on the page?

◉ Yes   ◉ No   Does the information provide in-depth coverage?

◉ Yes   ◉ No   Does the page provide links to other sites on the topic?

◉ Yes   ◉ No   Do the images, sound files, or videos add to the content?

◉ Yes   ◉ No   Does the site include a works cited or bibliography?

Explain why you would recommend this site to be included on our hotlist.

SUBMIT   CLEAR

Examples of Hotlists

Barley Sheaf School Library in Flemington, New Jersey
<http://www.frsd.k12.nj.us/barleylibrary/lib/student/cur.htm>
Davis High School Media Center in Kaysville, Utah
<http://dhs.davis.k12.ut.us/library/current.htm>

Promoting Hotlists and Curriculum Links

Direct students to hotlists and curriculum links as part of your information skills instruction. Students will realize the library's home page is their first resource if they are looking for quality Web sites for their assignments. Hotlists and curriculum links will not only generate publicity among students for the library program, but also among teachers. Publicize this service in your library's newsletters, at department and faculty meetings, and through e-mail. E-mail teachers examples of hotlists created by teachers in their department or subject area. This will highlight the valuable service that the library offers to both students and teachers.

Online Style Manual

One of the goals of the library's instructional program is to teach students to be effective users of ideas and information. The media specialist and teacher who collaboratively plan and teach the research process guide this journey of exploration and discovery. One aspect of this process is teaching students how to document the information they use in their research papers. The media specialist teaches the mechanics of the research process and guides the students as they document the sources used in their papers. To assist students with their research, many media specialists have created online style manuals for their students or posted links to online writing labs and style manuals. This presents another opportunity to publicize the library's instructional role in the school's curriculum. Students are instructed to consult the library's home page when they have questions about bibliographic format or citations. Each time a student uses the online style manual, the services the library provides are highlighted and promoted. This generates positive publicity for your program and for your role as an instructional leader.

Planning the Online Style Manual

Ideally, the process of creating a style manual should be shared with the language arts department. Create a committee of interested teachers to determine the content of the manual. Each member of the committee writes and edits a section of the manual while the media specialist is responsible for posting the manual to the library's home page.

The time frame for creating a manual varies depending on its content. Locating and posting links to writing labs and style manuals on your home page should only take a day or two. If you are limiting the manual to bibliographic and citation formats, allow at least a month to organize, type, and post the manual to your library's home page. However, if you are working with a committee to design a style manual for the entire research process, allow at least six months.

Content of the Online Style Manual

The research needs and ages of your students will determine the content of the style manual. You can include all the steps in the research process or just the format for citations and bibliographies. A good place to start is to post a style manual for bibliographies and citations. The formats for online databases are the most problematic for students; therefore, include examples of your library's databases in the manual. This will make your students' research lives much easier and will generate positive feedback and good-will for your library.

Design Considerations for the Online Style Manual

If you are working with a committee to write the style manual, have members save their work in an .HTML format. This will make it easier for you to cut and paste the text into your Web-authoring program.

Since you want your students to easily locate the style manual, place a link to it on a prominent place on your home page. Next, determine the organizational structure for the manual. You can make the manual easy to use by organizing the content as a list that is the manual's first page and the table of contents (see Figure 3.3). Make sure to include navigational links on each page of the manual so students can find their way back to the manual's table of contents and the index of the home page. Finally, adhere to the guidelines used in setting up your home page and keep the same format, colors, and graphics.

Examples of Online Style Manuals

Haddon Heights High School Library in Haddon Heights, New Jersey
<http://hhsd.k12.nj.us/library/workscited.htm>
Lakeland High School Library in Shrub Oak, New York
<http://www.lakelandschools.org/Libraries/LHSLib/webpage.html>
Selah Middle School Library in Selah, Washington
<http://share3.esd105.wednet.edu/mccayb/UsingRightCite.htm>

Style Manuals and Research Guides on the Web

If you are going to locate and post links to writing labs and style manuals on your home page, create a new category called research paper resources as part of the English subject heading links or on the index of your home page. There are many sites on the Internet to guide your students in the research process.

MLA Style Manual
<http://www.mla.org>
APA Style Manual
<http://www.apa.org>
OWL, the Online Writing Lab of Purdue University
<http://owl.english.purdue.edu>
Noodle Tools
Forms for generating works cited, which is a fee-based service.
<http://www.noodletools.com>

Promoting the Online Style Manual

It is important to work with the teachers and administrators in your school to designate the manual as the official research guide for students. This guarantees that teachers refer their classes to the manual and the library's home page when they have questions about documenting their research. Reinforce the importance of the online manual in the research process by directing students to it whenever they have a question about biblio-graphic format, and include it as part of every information skills lesson that you teach.

Figure 3.3   Sample Format for an Online Style Manual

Online Style Manual

Table of Contents

The Research Process

Thesis Statement

Sample Bibliography Cards

Examples of Bibliographic Entries

Sample Note Cards

Works Cited

The Outline

Note Taking

Parenthetical Citations

Sample Research Paper

Back

This service will definitely promote your library and your role as an information specialist to your students.

Ask a Librarian

A reference service that is increasingly making its way to libraries' home pages is a virtual reference desk, called Ask a Librarian, that provides homework assistance to students long after the library is closed. This homework assistance usually involves questions about books that were used in the library, citing sources, and the location of resources for an assignment. Answering these questions is a natural extension to homework and reference help provided on your home page and in your library. Ask a librarian is a service that will generate goodwill and promote your program as you come to the rescue of your frantic students and their parents after the library is closed for the day.

Planning Ask a Librarian

Ask a Librarian is a virtual reference center available around the clock, but this doesn't mean that you have to sit up all night waiting to respond to students' questions. Most media specialists include a notice on their Ask a Librarian page stating that the students will receive a response to their question within 24 hours. If you are going to include Ask a Librarian on your home page, decide whether to limit this service to students within your own school or district or to answer all questions that are submitted. Realistically, you will not have time to answer all questions submitted from outside of your school or district. In fact, this is a service that public libraries already provide to their patrons. Put a disclaimer on your page stating that this service is limited to students from your school or district. Next, decide the type of questions that you will answer and remind your students that you are not going to do their homework for them. Finally, allot time in your already overscheduled day to answer questions submitted to ask a librarian. It is a good idea to try to answer questions first thing in the morning or before you leave school for the day.

Design Considerations for Ask a Librarian

Locate the category for your Ask a Librarian service in a prominent place on the index of your home page, where your students can easily find this homework help. Include your name on the page because you want to personalize this service and let your students know who is answering their questions after the library is closed. After you have created a category on your home page entitled ask a librarian, provide instructions on using the service. This information should

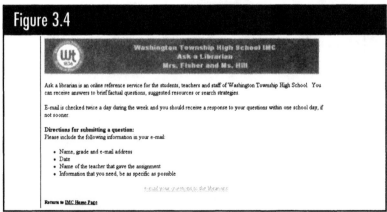

Washington Township High School in Sewell, New Jersey

include the name of the library, the purpose of the service, the restrictions on use, type of questions to be submitted, and response time to questions (see Figure 3.4).

Next, decide whether to provide this service using an e-mail link or a form. If you are going to set up an e-mail link, include this on the instruction page. An e-mail format is very easy for your students to use because all they do is click on the e-mail link and submit their questions. There are three disadvantages to using an e-mail format: you won't know if the question is being posed by your students or by someone else using the Internet; you will have to manually keep track of the number of questions received by Ask a Librarian; and students may not include all the information that you requested in the directions.

On the other hand, forms enable you to identify who is submitting the question, and to restrict access to students in your own school or district by requiring that students submit their student ID number. Forms assure that students will provide enough background information for you to answer their questions. Forms are not difficult to create and are available as part of most Web-authoring programs or on the Internet through a site called Forms.com. The main drawback to forms is that they require more time to complete because students are required to provide more information than just their question (see Figure 3.5).

Examples of Ask a Librarian Forms

Oswego High School Media Center in Oswego, New York
<http://www.oswego.org/staff/lcataldo/web/ask_a_librarian.htm>
Greece Athena Media Center in Rochester, New York
<http://www.greece.k12.ny.us/ath/library/askalibrarian/default.htm>

Examples of Ask a Librarian E-mail

DeKalb High School Library Media Center in DeKalb, Illinois
<http://www.dist428.dekalb.k12.il.us/dhs/services/media/home.html>
Wake Forest-Rolesville Middle School Media Center in Wake Forest, Illinois
<http://wfrms.wcpss.net/MediaCenter/Web_directory.html>

Promoting Ask a Librarian

Since this is a reference service, include information on using ask a librarian as part of your information skills lesson with each class that uses the library. When students begin using this service and realize they will get answers to their questions, they will spread the word and become your best advertisement.

Showcasing Student Projects

Media specialists display student work in the library to recognize student achievement in a visual display of the collaborative effort between the classroom teacher and the media specialist. Displaying student work also promotes the library and its instructional role to teachers, students, administrators, and parents. It is a good advertisement for your program. Traditionally, these displays were housed on the library's bulletin boards, walls, and display cases so everyone in the school could see them. Now, with a link on your library home page and a click of the mouse, student work can be displayed to a world-wide audience.

Figure 2.4   Ask a Librarian Form

Ask a Librarian
Mrs. Smith

Ask a Librarian is an online reference service for the students, teachers and staff of Happy High School. You can receive answers to brief factual questions, suggested resources or search strategies.

E-mail is checked twice a day during the week and you should receive a response to your question within one school day, if not sooner.

Your Name

Student ID

E-mail Address

Teacher's Name

Submit your question; be as specific as possible.

Back to Main Page

SUBMIT   CLEAR

Planning Student Project Pages

There are not enough days in the school year to display all student work that results from research in the library. A good place to begin is to display those assignments that were collaboratively planned and taught in the library. The work that is best showcased on the library's home page includes multimedia presentations, Web pages, and research papers because they can be saved in an .HTML format, which allows you to cut and paste the projects into your Web-authoring programs. Therefore, displaying student work on your home page will not take very much time. The responsibility for showcasing student work is shared. First, the teacher determines the criteria for selecting student work because, realistically, the quality of student work is not necessarily the same. Second, the teacher is responsible for saving all files in an .HTML format and giving them to the media specialist by a predetermined date. Third, the media specialist instructs the students on the importance of following copyright laws and adhering to the district's Web publishing guidelines, while the teacher verifies that the students have followed these policies. Finally, the media specialist posts the projects to the library's home page.

Design Considerations for Student Project Pages

There are two ways to post student work to the library's home page. If you have a teacher assignment page, it seems logical to post student work there with the requirements of the assignment. Just add a link called student projects and create a list or table of the projects by student name or by the name of the work. If you don't have a teacher assignment page, then create a category called student projects on the index of your library's home page, and organize these projects into an alphabetical list or table by the teacher's name or class. Just a reminder, if you are using students' names, follow your district's Web publishing policy.

Use the same format and colors on the student project page as used on the home page. Use navigation links to direct students back to the index of the home page.

Examples of Student Project Pages

North Crowley High School Library in Crowley, Texas
<http://www.crowley.k12.tx.us/chp/nchs/library>
Buckley Elementary School Media Center in Lansing, New York
<http://www.lansingschools.org/les/library>
Ithaca High School Media Center in Ithaca, New York
<http://www.icsd.k12.ny.us/highschool/library/>
Craig High School Library Media Center in Janesville, Wisconsin
<http://www.inwave.com/schools/Craig/library/index.html>

Promoting Student Project Pages

These student projects can be advertised at your school's open house and through your PTA. You really won't have to work very hard to promote this section of your home page because students will spread the word. They like seeing their work displayed online and will show their friends and parents their accomplishments. Showcasing student work is another excellent advertisement for your library's instructional program.

Virtual Tours

As media specialists, we are always looking for innovative ways to package an orientation that hold students' interest and provides an overview of library services and procedures. A virtual tour of your library allows you to merge the students' love of computers with the goal of introducing them to your library. Students use the library's home page to begin their virtual tour, where they learn about staff and hours, procedures, services, and the collection. A virtual tour link on your home page will engage your students in learning about the services of the library and will generate positive feelings towards the library among your new students. The virtual tour can even be used to publicize your services to parents during back-to-school night. When the parents visit the library, direct them to the home page and the virtual tour where they can share the same library experiences as their child.

Content of Virtual Tours
The virtual tour is an opportunity to showcase your library to your new students and can include the following:
- Staff and the services they provide to students
- Hours of operation and procedures for using the library during and after school
- Procedures including rules, borrowing privileges, circulation periods, library cards, and fines
- The district's Internet and computer policy
- The print and electronic collection

Use the virtual tour to highlight any special features of your library. For example, include information on the number of computers available to students, interlibrary loan programs, or remote access for reference databases and the library catalog. Consider including a virtual quiz to test the students' understanding of the library's services and procedures.

Design Considerations for Virtual Tours
Make your virtual tour visibly attractive by illustrating the text with pictures of the staff, teachers, and students using the services of the library. For example, begin the virtual tour with a picture of smiling students entering the library. This is a promotional image for your new students to see—students who love coming to the library. Another stop on the virtual tour is a description of the print resources available to students. Here, use pictures of students reading books, magazines, and newspapers. Use a digital camera to take your pictures as this allows you to insert them directly into your Web-authoring program. Save your pictures as a .jpeg or .gif file and keep the size of the file small because the pages will load more quickly. Also, use different colors, fonts, and backgrounds to keep the tour visually exciting.

Next, decide the organizational structure for the virtual tour. After you create a category for the virtual tour on your home page, use a list for each section. The order of the list is based on the priority of each service that your library provides. A good suggestion is to begin the virtual tour by introducing the staff because these are the people who will assist the students with their research.

Finally, it is extremely important to include navigational tools that are highly visible so students can return to the various sections of the virtual tour and the index of the home page. If you are going to use icons, include the text descriptions so it is accessible to special needs students.

Examples of Virtual Tours

Congress Middle School Media Center in Palm Beach, Florida
<http://www.palmbeach.k12.fl.us/CongressMS/Student_Media_
Center_Pages/Linsey_Danny/html%20files/Media_home.htm>
Hillsborough High School in Hillsborough, New Jersey
<http://www.hillsborough.k12.nj.us/hhs/tempx/default.htm>
Coral Gables Senior High School Media Center in Coral Gables, Florida
<http://cghs.dade.k12.fl.us/library/tour/tour.htm>

Promoting Virtual Tours

The virtual tour needs no promotion with your students because they will take the tour as part of their orientation program. Use the tour to introduce transfer students to your library's services and ask parents to take the virtual tour during back-to-school night. This is an excellent means to publicize your program to the community at large and to build bridges that can only benefit the library program.

Community Outreach

Introduction

It is important to publicize library programs that support student academic success to taxpayers because their support is necessary for libraries to thrive. Your library's home page becomes a showcase to promote your programs and services and in doing so, it expands the role of the school library to include a community beyond the school's walls. It also provides an opportunity to forge partnerships within the community, from the families of the students you teach, to the public library, to the Chamber of Commerce, and to community groups, such as senior citizens.

Parents and the Library

An important component to students' academic success is parental involvement in the school. Parents want to be involved in their children's education, but their job schedules often conflict with school hours, thus making it very difficult for them to meet with their children's teachers to discuss assignments, and to find enough time to help their children with their homework. In addition, many parents don't have the time to research information issues such as copyright, plagiarism, and Internet safety that face their children. A home page fosters a connection between parents and the school library and at the same time promotes the library's programs and services.

Planning the Parent Page
Schedule a meeting with the Parent Teacher Association (PTA) leadership and gather ideas for a parents' section for your home page. Ask about issues that concern parents and discuss the home page and how it can be a useful tool for them. Another way to determine the content of your parent page is to design a survey of issues that interest parents, such as dress codes, drugs and alcohol, child safety on the net, and filtering

software. Distribute this survey during back-to-school night. The survey results will help determine the content for your parent page. Also, contact your school administrative office for demographic information about your school and your community. For example, if demographics demonstrate that your community has a large multi-ethnic population, your home page can address their needs by offering your home page in more than one language.

Content of the Parent Page

The content of the parent page serves as an academic portal to the library's services and resources. It should complement and not compete with the district's or PTA's home pages; therefore, don't publish lunch menus, school calendars, PTA events, or fundraisers that are usually on those pages. Do include the following on your parent page:

- An overview and aim of the library program.
- Technology and educational issues facing parents, schools, and children such as plagiarism and copyright issues, Internet use and safety, computers and learning.
- A copy of the district's acceptable use policy (AUP) and a letter to parents regarding Internet use.
- Parenting skill sites, which include sites for single parents, help with adolescents, and links to the National Institute of Health site and other sites dealing with psychiatric disorders affecting children and adolescents.
- Homework help sites—be sure to remind parents that your home page has the best curriculum sites on the Internet.
- A link to a virtual tour of the library so that parents can familiarize themselves with what is available in the library, including print, non-print, and Web-based resources.
- If non-English speakers make up a large segment of the schools' population, provide links to assist them, such as ESL links, and links specific to the language spoken in your community.
- Links to full e-text of classics that are now in the public domain such as Project Guttenberg. <http://promo.net/pg/>
- A link from the home page to the district's PTA site is useful to newcomers to the community who would like to find information about the organization. If the district Web page does not provide a calendar of events for parents, include this on your home page. It will help parents plan their calendar according to the school calendar of events.
- Links to consumer information such as *Kelley's Blue Book* and *Consumer Reports* and other sites that provide reviews and recommendations for automobiles, home electronics, and other household goods as well as information on health, fitness, sports, and recreation.
- Link to the Forms/Survey section of your home page so parents can access missing letters and forms that were sent home.

Design Considerations for the Parent Page

Come up with an eye-catching name for this section of your home page such as Parents' Place or Parents' Info Line. You have several options in placing the links on your home page. You can list the parent page as another link on the index of your home page, but the problem here is that it may get lost among the links. Another option is to display the site using a button, which runs at the top of the page, just under the library's name (see Figure 4.1). Finally, you can use photographs; just make sure to keep the file small and use a .jpeg or .gif format, so the page does not take too long to download. Whichever style you choose, be consistent in the format for displaying your links. This also applies to colors and fonts. Remember to include navigational links from this page to your curriculum page and back to your index page because the parents will also be using the curriculum links for homework help.

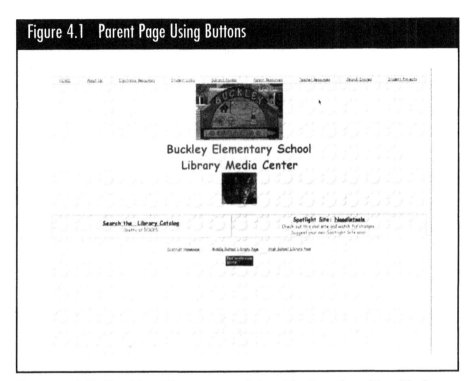

Figure 4.1   Parent Page Using Buttons

Raymond E. Buckley Elementary School in Lansing, New York

Examples of Parent Pages

Castro Valley High School Cybrary in Castro Valley, California
<http://www.homework-central.com/schools/CVHSCybrary/main.html>
Buckley Elementary School in Lansing, New York
<http://www.lansingschools.org/les/library>
Meyers Library in Wyncote, Pennsylvania
<http://www.ancillae.org/library/>
Congress Middle School in Palm Beach, Florida
<http://www.palmbeach.k12.fl.us/congressms/media.html>
Edinburg High School in Edinburg, Texas
<http://www.edinburg.cisd.tenet.edu/campuses/ehs2/LIBRARY/EHS
Library.htm>
St. Joseph's Nudgee College in QLD, Australia
<http://www.nudgee.com/library/>
Dr. George M. Weir Library in British Columbia, Canada
<http://weir.vsb.bc.ca/library/parents.html>

Richmond High School Library in New South Wales, Australia
<http://www.geocities.com/richmondnsw/STAFF/family.html>
James S. Wilson Middle School Library in Erie, Pennsylvania
<http://www.mtsd.org/jswilson/main/library/plinks.html>
Chico High School in Chico, California
<http://dewey.chs.chico.k12.ca.us/>

Promoting the Parent Page

Promote this section of your home page by advertising it in the principal's newsletter, which is distributed to the community. Hosting a PTA meeting in the library should follow this, so parents can see the library as well as its home page. Attend a back-to-school night to plug your home page to all of the parents in the school district.

Home Schooling

According to a survey published by Patricia M. Lines in *Homeschoolers: Estimating Numbers and Growth*, home schooling has risen from 360,000 students in 1994 to 850,000 in 2000 and is rapidly approaching a million. Your library's home page can provide resources to this growing group of parents and students. Planning this home schooling page will not take very much time because your home page already provides resources designed to meet the curriculum standards for your state. Anyone who has an Internet connection can access these resources; all you will need to do is send the home schoolers in your community your library's URL and directions on how to access this information on your home page. You can obtain their addresses from your school district office, as all home schoolers have to be registered with the school district. You will be providing a valuable service to these parents and students and at the same time highlighting your library's services and resources to another segment of the community's population.

Content of the Home Schooling Page

Point home schoolers to the curriculum links, the online catalog, online databases, and other sites which are already part of your home page. Make it easy and convenient for home schooling parents to locate resources they can use to educate their children by including the following links:

- Electronic texts, such as links to e-text such as Project Guttenberg. This site allows the parents to have access to public domain books. <http://promo.net/pg/>
- MLA and APA online style manuals. If your library has an online style manual, be sure to refer parents to it because it is designed for students and geared to the curriculum.
- If your home page has online brochures that provide step-by-step instructions on searching the online catalog and databases, make sure that a link is provided for these.
- The Internet has some exceptional tutorials on Windows, Searching the Web, PowerPoint, FrontPage, Publisher, and Word. Post these sites so students can learn how to use these applications. If you have designed tutorials for your students and staff, post these as well.

- Post a bibliography on home schooling.
- Post home schooling sites that are designed specifically for home schooling. These pages provide access to state laws, resources, support groups, and discussion groups. Most are free, but some charge a fee.

Jon's Home School Resource Page
<http://www.midnightbeach.com/hs/Web_Pages.res.f.html>

The Home School Legal Defense Fund site provides information on state laws and organizations listed by state.
<http://www.hslda.org/hs/default.asp>

LearningPlanet is a fee-based site that provides online activities and curriculum organized by grade level.
<http://www.learningplanet.com/index.asp>

Home School Resource Page
<http://www.hsu.edu/faculty/worthf/hs.html>

The Home Schooling Conferences site lists upcoming conferences, conventions, and fairs.
<http://www.sound.net/~ejcol/confer.html>

The Virtual Chalkboard is a guide to home schooling.
<http://www.spiral-web.com/Education_Directory/homeschool.htm>

National Home Education Research Institute
<http://www.nheri.org>

The Home School
<http://thehomeschool.freeyellow.com>

Home Education Magazine offers newsletters, discussion forums, and networking.
<http://home-ed-magazine.com/index.html>

Learn In Freedom offers information about college for home schooled students as well as many links to Web sites that deal with independent learning.
<http://learninfreedom.org/>

The Education Research Information Center (ERIC) site provides information on home schooling.
<http://www.indiana.edu/~eric_rec/comatt/ghome.html>

Design Considerations for the Home Schooling Page

There are two ways to locate the link for your home schooling page: a link on your parent page; or a separate category on your library's home page. Either way, explain the purpose of the page and provide your library's address and e-mail so parents can contact you. This page should not take too long to design because you are using the resources already available on your home page and adding sites that pertain to home schooling.

Promoting the Home Schooling Page

Since home schoolers have to register with local school districts, obtain their names and addresses from your superintendent's office and mail them information about your home page. Include the URL of your library's home page, an explanation of the educational sites available to them, login information, passwords, and your name and e-mail address.

Public Libraries

Communication is the first step toward a working relationship between the school library and public library. The school librarian has many roles that are integral to the school's curriculum, and the goal of these roles is to make sure that students can access, evaluate, and use information. Likewise, the public librarian's goal is to respond to the information needs of the community. Both school and public librarians share a common objective and that is to meet the information needs of students and to encourage them to read. Cooperation is the key word in this common quest.

Although this type of cooperation and collaboration has been traditionally encouraged through grants, your library's home page can extend this cooperation by providing access to the public library resources on your home page. This benefits the students, the public library, your school library, and the community while forging a partnership between the two libraries.

Content of the Public Library Page

Many school librarians have a virtual reference service called Ask a Librarian on their home page. Though this is a useful service for students, it has several drawbacks. There is a time delay in receiving a response to questions during the school year and this service is not available during the summer, on weekends, and during holidays. However, by providing a link to the public library's virtual reference desk, students can receive help in locating information when school is not in session and you are not available. Many public libraries have instituted virtual reference desks where librarians are available 24 hours a day, seven days a week to answer online reference questions. Therefore, the addition of this service to your home page requires no work; just the time spent linking to the public library that offers this service.

Many public libraries have their catalog online; this resource should be included on your home page as it will enable students to peruse the collection, put a book on hold, or reserve a book they need for their school research assignments. Your public library will also want to make the school library's catalog available on their home page, thus fostering collaboration between the two libraries.

Your home page can also be used to build a partnership with the public library through reading promotion. Post your school's summer reading list on both home pages and include the titles that are available in both libraries. Use your home page to advertise the public library's summer reading program and any other programs they conduct for children and teens.

Many public libraries hold programs for students such as karaoke parties, magic nights, visiting author nights, orchestra nights, mystery nights, and other programs. Posting these activities on your home page is another way to collaborate with the public library.

Design Considerations for the Public Library Page

Create a link on the index of your home page entitled other libraries (see Figure 4.2). Make this page visually exciting by using photos, graphics, and varying fonts. Since you are collaborating with your community's public library, one of the first things that the students should see is the name and photograph of the library. Make a personal connection for your students with the public library's staff by including a group photo of the staff with their names and short biographies. Keep students interested in this section by including a virtual bulletin board display of photos of your students using the public library, since students enjoy looking at photos of their peers.

Figure 4.2 Location of Link for Other Libraries

Other Libraries

Alameda County	Haystar (CSU Hayward)	UC Berkeley	Library of Congress

Online Periodicals

Electric Library Free School Cal.	News Resources (Online Newspapers and News Services)	Full-text Magazine Database

Local Info

Castro Valley	Bay	California

General Research

Career and College Links Teen Topics	Information Please Online Web Searchers	Research & Writing Homework Central

Resources by Department

English & ESL Mathematics Physical Education	Foreign Language Science Visual and Performing Arts	Health Social Studies Vocational/Technical

Ethnic Links

African	Asian/Pacific	European	Latino	Native

Castro Valley Cybrary in Castro Valley, California

In addition to providing links directly to the home pages of libraries in your area, link directly to your public library's virtual reference service, their online catalog, and information about their summer reading programs and other events. Promote the public library's special events by running a banner across the index page of your school library's home page. Follow the same format, font, colors, and design considerations that you used with the other sections of your home page.

Examples of Public Library Pages

Castro Valley High School Cybrary in Castro Valley, California
<http://www.homework-central.com/schools/CVHSCybrary/main.html>
Bonita High School in La Verne, California
<http://www.bonita.k12.ca.us/bonita/library/index.html>
Redwood High School in Redwood City, California
<http://rhsweb.org/library/>
Mother Teresa Catholic Secondary School in Ontario, Canada
<http://ldcsb.on.ca/schools/mths/>
Concord Elementary School in Anderson, South Carolina
<http://concord.anderson5.net/library>
The Edna M. Fielder Elementary School in Katy, Texas
<http://www.katy.isd.tenet.edu/fe/library/fielderlibrary/
fielderlibrary.html>

Promoting the Public Library Page

Advertise the public library section of your home page when you conduct orientation classes for incoming students and each time you teach information skills classes. Provide the local public library with brochures and bookmarks about your library.

Senior Citizens

Many media specialists already are involved in community outreach to senior citizens by offering technology workshops, which promote partnerships between students and seniors and strengthen ties between school libraries and the senior community. A natural extension of this outreach is a resource page and online computer courses designed for senior citizens by media specialists and students. Working with older members of the community will enable students to understand the special needs of senior citizens and will generate a positive image for young adults in the community. It will also have the added benefit of informing the community that the school library is a valuable resource, a very important factor at budget time.

Planning the Senior Citizen Page

This is an activity for your student advisory board, student assistants, or community service organization. Since the senior citizen page is a student activity, one of the first things you will have to do is determine the areas of responsibility. Students are responsible for the design, content, and maintenance of the page. As their advisor, you are responsible for supervising the students, organizing the meetings, and creating the page. This activity will be very time consuming in the beginning as you work with students to get the senior citizen page off the ground. To save yourself time, collaborate with your school's computer club or Webmaster and have them publish the page.

Hold an organizational meeting for interested students and include the following items on your agenda. Review the district's Web publishing policy so students will know the district's guidelines for publishing on the Web. Determine the areas of responsibility for students, the school's computer club, and the advisor. Develop a tentative timetable for completing the page. Finally, set up a meeting schedule.

At subsequent meetings, students will be assigned content areas of the senior citizen page. These assignments should be based on personal preference and areas of expertise. Emphasize that it is extremely important for students to maintain the sites that are in their content area. Let them know as their advisor, you are responsible for the content of the resource pages and that means you will review the sites that have been selected. This can be accomplished during regular meetings.

Content of the Senior Citizen Page

The goal of this home page is to provide Web-based resources for your community's senior citizens. In deciding the content of the page, students should have an understanding of the special needs of senior citizens. To accomplish this, invite a local representative of AARP, a geriatric specialist, or a retirement community administrator to one of your meetings.

The content of the senior citizen page can include links to health information, senior citizen organizations such as AARP, local community resources and special events, government agencies such as the Social Security Administration, leisure activities and travel, retirement planning, genealogy, and free e-mail sites.

Design Considerations for the Senior Citizen Page

Place the link to the senior citizen page on the index page of your home page. Use the same design rules used for your library's home page for the senior citizen page. Maintain a consistent format using the same colors and graphics; however, increase the font size to at least 14 points; this will make it easier to read. Always include navigational tools, so users can easily return from the table of contents of the senior citizen page to the index of the library's home page. Organize the content as an alphabetical table to display the categories. This will enable the seniors to easily review the contents of the page without scrolling.

Post your e-mail address so senior citizens can send useful links, notify you when links no longer work, and offer suggestions to improve their home page. This will give senior citizens a voice in the project.

Online Computer Literacy Courses for Senior Citizens

As part of community outreach, many school media specialists offer computer courses in their libraries after school. Senior citizens love attending these computer courses, but because budget constraints often limit enrollment, they may not always be able to attend. Utilize your home page to offer these courses online. There are numerous advantages to offering these courses online to senior citizens: they work at their own pace; they don't have to worry about making arrangements to get to the school library; and they are free. Every time a senior citizen clicks on your home page to take an online course, your library's services and resources have a positive impact in the community.

Content of the Senior Citizen Online Courses

Computer literacy is a useful information resource for senior citizens. The following are examples of online courses to offer senior citizens.

- *The Basic Computer Literacy Course* covers computer terminology, parts of the computer, printing, and saving files.
- *The Mouse Course* covers the basic concepts of scrolling, pointing, and clicking.
- *The Searching the World Wide Web Course* introduces seniors to search engines, directories, and metasearch engines and well as search strategies. Includes a glossary of technology terms and information dealing with hoaxes, viruses, and spam.
- *The Introduction to E-mail Course* covers the basic concepts of e-mail, sending and receiving e-mail, and sites to acquire free e-mail accounts.

You don't have to actually design these courses yourself. There are some excellent tutorials on the Internet that you can post to your senior citizen page.

Examples of Tutorials
- Mousercise: Chris Ripple from The Central Kansas Library System designed both tutorials.
  < http://www.ckls.org/~crippel/computerlab/tutorials/mouse/page1.html>
- KeyBoard
  <http://www.ckls.org/~crippel/computerlab/tutorials/keyboard/page1.html>
- Welcome to the Web was designed by Steve Garwood of Camden County Library in Voorhees, New Jersey.
  <http://reference.camden.lib.nj.us/classes/garwood/welcome2web/>

Provide senior citizens with the opportunity to ask questions and voice concerns regarding the content of the online workshops. E-mail is an expedient way to answer their questions. If they do not have e-mail, give them your voice mail number. Let them know that you will get back to them on the same day that you receive the e-mail or voice mail.

Design Considerations for the Senior Citizen Online Courses
Create a link called online computer courses on your senior citizen page. Be sure to include your e-mail address and voice mail number with a reminder that you will answer any questions they have regarding the courses. Follow the same guidelines that you used in designing your senior citizen page and annotate each link for the online courses. This annotation should include a description of the workshop, prerequisites, and other information that would be helpful to senior citizens.

Promoting the Senior Citizen Page and Online Computer Courses
You can reach a large segment of your community's senior citizens by contacting local senior citizen organizations and retirement communities and asking them to post brochures and distribute flyers. You can also publicize the home page at computer workshops for senior citizens that are given in your library or in your district.

Community Resources

Many local communities have immeasurable resources of culture, history, and services. However, in some cases, information about local assets is not conveniently found in one place, thereby making it very difficult to quickly locate information about the community and its resources and services.

Take a proactive approach and make all of these resources easily and quickly available on your library's home page. This will promote your library as a valuable benefit for residents who will come to rely on your home page for information about their community.

Content of the Community Resources Page
The content of the community resources page should reflect the personality of the community where your school library is located. There is so much information that can be included in this section of your home page that the individual makeup of a community will dictate the priority of what should or should not be included. This is not a one-size-fits-all page.

The following are examples of resources to post on your community resources page.

- Community Recreation—This can be anything from sports leagues to hiking trails. Make it easy for the community to get specific information about the recreation opportunities by listing the phone number, address, contact person, and e-mail address for each opportunity.
- Community Events—Provide a description of the events along with the dates and times. If there is a contact person, be sure to include that on your page.
- School, Academic, and Public Libraries—List the libraries' addresses, hours of operation, contact names, e-mail addresses, and phone numbers. Provide a link to their home pages.
- Continuing Education Courses—These are usually offered through your local school district and community colleges; include a link to the section of their home page which lists their course offerings.
- Community Help Organization—Provide links to drug and alcohol counseling, suicide prevention, and other psychological and trauma counseling agencies. Include the name, address, and phone number for each contact person. Be sure to include a disclaimer that you are not endorsing or promoting these organizations.
- Health and Wellness Organizations—List links to local hospitals, fitness centers, medical sites such as the National Institute of Health, and other sites dealing with information on health and disease. Be sure to include a disclaimer that you are not endorsing or promoting these organizations.
- Consumer Information—Include links to sites such as *Consumer Reports* and *Kelley's Blue Book.*
- News Stories—If there is an ongoing local, national, or international special interest story, post links to the story and online maps to pinpoint its location. This will enable the community to quickly access information about the story using your home page. You can also provide a list of books that relate to this event.
- Local and State Government—Connect the user directly to the home pages of these government resources.
- Ready References Resources—Online maps, almanacs, and *Bartlett's Book of Quotations* are also helpful additions for questions that may pop up at any time of the day or night.
- Genealogy—Genealogical sites are always popular for those interested in local history as well as for those searching for information about their ancestors.
- Investment Sites.
- Weather Information.
- Entertainment—Provide the addresses and phone numbers for movie houses, theaters, and museums. If you are really ambitious, you can include their programs and update it on a weekly basis. Provide a link to their home pages, if available.
- Book Donations—If you live in a community that allots an inadequate book budget for your school library, your home page is a good place to solicit new books from the community. People could use special events such as Mother's Day, birthdays, anniversaries, and other important dates (see Figure 4.3) to donate a book to the school library. The library would recognize this donation by inserting a bookplate in the inside cover of the book with the name of the donor and list the title of the book and its donor's name on your home page.

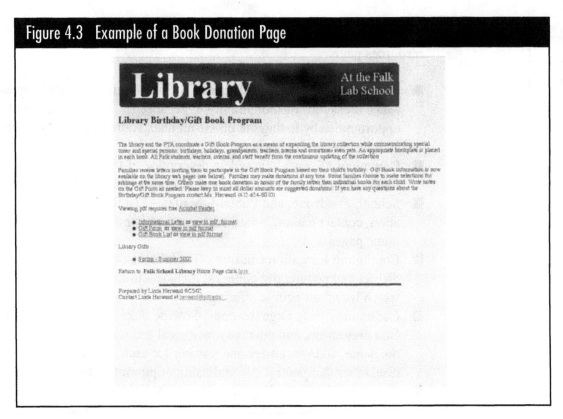

Figure 4.3 Example of a Book Donation Page

Falk School Library in Pittsburgh, Pennsylvania

Design Considerations for the Community Resources Page

Display your community resources page prominently on your home page as this allows the community to quickly locate this page. Ideally, the best location is on the index of your home page directly below your library's name (see Figure 4.4). You can simply call the link community resources or you can be very creative and use an image map that combines the title of the page with a photograph of a well-known community landmark.

As mentioned earlier, remember to keep the picture files small and save graphics as .jpegs or .gifs so the page loads quickly. Also, follow the same design format as your other pages. Display the community information as either an alphabetical list or a table, as this will make it easier to locate the resources. Include your e-mail address so members of the community can give you feedback on the community resources page.

Examples of Community Resources Pages

Castro Valley High School in Castro Valley, California
<http://www.homework-central.com/schools/CVHSCybrary/main.html>

North Crowley High School in Forth Worth, Texas
<http://www.crowley.k12.tx.us/chp/nchs/library/>

Chico High School in Chico, California
<http://dewey.chs.chico.k12.ca.us/>

Fayetteville High School in Fayetteville, Arkansas
<http://fayar.net/east/library/>

Clinton High School in Clinton, Tennessee
<http://www.acorns.k12.tn.us/schools/clintonh/local.htm>

Falk Laboratory School Library in Pittsburgh, Pennsylvania
<http://tc.education.pitt.edu/library/index.html>

Figure 4.4   Location of Community Resources

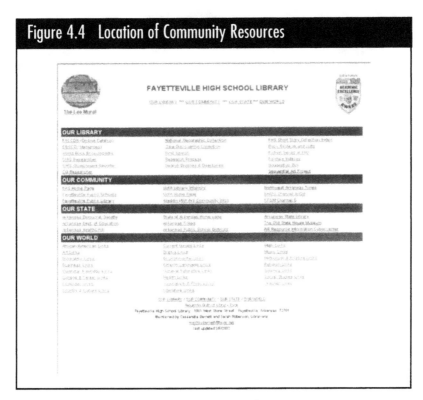

Fayetteville High School in Fayetteville, Arkansas

Promoting the Community Resources Page

Collaborate with your public relations office to design announcements that will appear on radio and television to advertise community resources and information on your library's home page. Be sure to include the URL and a contact person in your announcement. Invite a local newspaper reporter to write an article about the home page. Attend and speak at a municipal or borough hall meeting. Provide the community in attendance with a brochure about your home page and tell them what type of information is posted there. Ask for feedback on the page and ask them to e-mail you with their comments and recommendations.

Chapter Five

Promotional Strategies

Introduction

There are many activities you do every day that can be used to promote your library program. All you have to do is get the word out. The best way to do that is to create a long-term advocacy campaign, which creates an image in the minds of administrators, teachers, students, and the community that the library is an indispensable and invaluable resource.

The thrust of this promotional campaign is short-term activities that showcase the services and programs that you do every day. These activities emanate from your mission statement, your goals, and your library's services and programs. In marketing terms, you are going to create a media blitz—a non-stop advertising campaign that highlights your media program.

To get this campaign started, make a list of all the activities you do every day. This list should include teaching information skills classes, researching for teachers and administrators, compiling Web sites, maintaining a Web page, budgeting, ordering, conducting book talks, collaborating with teachers, organizing pathfinders, writing newsletters and brochures—the list is endless. You probably view many of these activities as just something you do every day to provide exemplary service to students and teachers, but these "routine" activities are going to form the cornerstone of your advocacy campaign.

The following section describes how you can showcase your every day activities on your home page as part of your ongoing promotional campaign to highlight your library program.

Newsletters

As a promotional tool, newsletters are a proactive approach in communicating to teachers and administrators on a continuing basis the activities taking place in the library. You probably write a print newsletter each month to promote your library and its programs. Now, you can transform that print newsletter into a Web-based delivery system that communicates your programs to the school community. Posting your newsletter to your Web page will probably take less time than the print version because you won't have to copy and distribute it in your teachers' mailboxes.

Content of the Newsletters

One of your first considerations should be the number of issues you want to publish electronically each year. Since a Web-based newspaper is no more time-consuming than print, start with the same number of issues.

Next, decide the information you want to communicate and how you can capture the reader's attention. The best way to do this is to make the newsletter teacher oriented, since they are your primary audience. The writing style should be informal, but informative. Keep the articles short and to the point; you don't want waste your teachers and administrators' time. Remember that the front page of the newsletter is the first thing teachers and administrators will see; you want to entice them to continue reading. So, use articles that will interest them.

The content of the newsletters can include information on library programs and activities, technology tips, new arrivals, online databases, book reviews, and information on classes and teachers using the library. Include articles that relate to the seasons of the school year; for example, since many teachers like to travel, the last issue of the year should include travel sites. Just as newspapers have sections devoted to specific topics, do the same thing with the newsletter. Place your featured columns in the same place in every issue so teachers will learn to look for them. For example, a technology help section might be a featured column.

If you want to know how many teachers and administrators are reading the newsletter, make it interactive by including a response mechanism. These mechanisms include online contests, surveys, and a suggestion box. Offer a gift or prize for responding to the contest or survey. You can also include a counter or a Web statistics program on your newsletter so you will know that it is being read. These counters are found in most Web-authoring programs or you can download a free counter at the following sites:

Analog
> <http://www.analog.cx/>

Site Meter
> <http://sm6.sitemeter.com/default.asp>

NedStat
> <http://www.nedstat.com/usa/f80012_index.htm>

Design Considerations for Newsletters

Using a template for your electronic newsletters will save time and promote consistency from issue to issue. The template should have a banner with your library's name and logo, volume number, issue number and date, a table of contents, and links to back issues.

Newsletters are usually 8 by 11 inches in size and use a multicolumn format—you can use one, two, or three column formats on the same page. A frames format of two columns (see Figure 5.1) works well. The left frame is about one-fifth the width of the newsletter and includes the table of contents, links to back issues, and links to current articles. The right frame takes up four-fifths of the publication; this frame displays the articles.

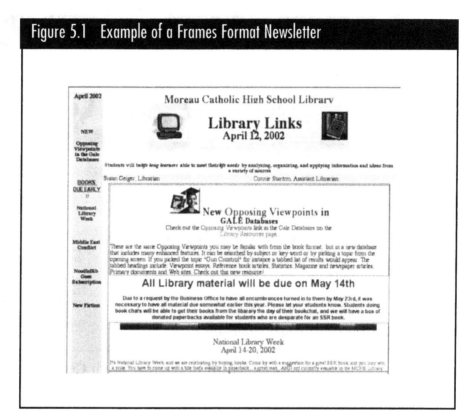

Figure 5.1   Example of a Frames Format Newsletter

Moreau Catholic High School Library in Haywood, California

Don't fill every space with text or graphics; you don't want the page to appear crowded. Use less text and break up lists with bulleted heading or subheadings. Graphics can make the newsletter eye-catching, but they should support the text. Limit the number of graphics and keep the file size small, so the page loads quickly. Most online newsletters set a two-page limit. Also, proofread, proofread, proofread—this eliminates spelling and grammar errors and typos.

Finally, publish your online newsletter as a .pdf or .HTML file. A .pdf file is a universal file format that lets you view and print a document exactly as it looked when you designed it. There are advantages and disadvantages to both formats. The .HTML file is perfect for reading on a computer screen and it makes creating a newsletter archive very easy; just create an internal link to your newsletter files. As easy as this sounds, an .HTML newsletter doesn't look the same when printed. It loses some of its formatting. For example, the layout may become distorted. In contrast, a .pdf file has fewer design limitations; it looks exactly the same online as in print. It keeps its original colors, fonts, layout, and images. However, .pdf files have several disadvantages. You must purchase the Adobe Acrobat software and learn how to create documents with it.

The files are larger and take longer to download. Readers must have the .pdf software reader, Adobe Acrobat Reader, on their computers. If you decide to use a .pdf format be sure to include a link to Adobe Acrobat Reader with the newsletter so readers can download the software to their computers (see Figure 5.2). You can get this free software at <http://www.adfobe.com>.

Just put their logo on your newsletter and create a hyperlink to their site.

Figure 5.2   Example of a Newsletter That Uses a .pdf Format

September 5, 2001   Volume 6 Issue 1

MES Faculty and Staff,

Thank you to those who attended our first Media Center Moment last Thursday! I put a brochure about DISCUS databases in your box Friday to give you more information. Please ask questions about these resources. We can include online research when you are researching various topics.

As always, let us know how we can help.
The Media Center Staff—D & S

P. S. I finally figured out DISCUS means

Come By & Schedule a Visit to the Media Center
Teachers in 1st - 4th grade, come by at your convenience and schedule a lesson or storytime! Here are some ideas for lessons:

Call Numbers
Organization of Fiction Resources
Organization of Nonfiction—Dewey Decimal System

Using OPAC
    Title Search

Midway Media Center in Lexington, South Carolina

Last but not least, after you have created your newsletter, be sure to view it with commonly used browsers to see exactly how it will look, as you don't want to post it to your home page and discover that the pictures are too big or the newsletter looks distorted.

Examples of Newsletters
Moreau Catholic High School Library in Hayward, California
        <http://www.moreaucatholic.org/public/library/library.html>
Midway Media Center in Lexington, South Carolina
        <http://www.lexington1.net/mes/lmc/nuts.html>
Bessie Chin High School Library in Redwood, California
        <http://rhsweb.org/library/library_leaves.htm>
Arvin High School Library Media Center in Bakersfield, California
        <http://www.khsd.k12.ca.us/arvin>
Bonita High School Library in La Verne, California
        <http://www.bonita.k12.ca.us/schools/bonita/library/LibWebP12.html>

Promoting the Newsletters

Send e-mail to teachers, administrators, and staff announcing each new issue. Be sure to pique their interest by including one of the newsletter's headlines in your e-mail.

Brochures

Brochures are a fast and effective way to communicate information about specific library services. They are also a means of assisting teachers and students with information, and they highlight the library's program.

Posting brochures to your home page has numerous advantages. It will save time because you will no longer have to print them and put them in teachers' mailboxes. You can easily locate them when needed. Online brochures provide instant access to information so teachers, administrators, students, and parents can view the information whenever they want. The brochures are now available to a wider audience — anyone searching the Internet has access to the information in your brochures.

Content of the Brochures

A good way to start creating online brochures is to convert one of your print brochures into an electronic format. Eventually, you'll build up an archive of brochures on all aspects of library service.

In deciding the content of your brochures, stay focused on the type of information that your students and teachers need, such as Internet and online database searching. Also, target specific audiences. For example, you might want to create brochures describing the best online resources for teachers. You can also design the content around a specific theme such as books for teachers or students or National Library Week.

The following are content ideas for library brochures:

- Library Services
- Internet Search Strategies
- Introduction to the Library's Databases
- Promotional Events
- Special Programs
- Book Lists
- Pathfinders
- Frequently Asked Questions

The content of the brochures should be written in an informative tone using a minimum of words; keep it short and simple. The brochure should be easy to read and provide readers with the information they want in an engaging format.

Design Considerations for Brochures

The key word in designing brochures is simplicity. The brochure should be attractive and eye-catching, but the design should not overwhelm the information. Use the same template for all of your brochures; it will save time and it guarantees consistency in layout, colors, graphics, and fonts.

Design Techniques for Brochures

- Don't fill every space with text and graphics; you don't want the brochure to appear crowded.
- Use subheadings and bullets to break up the text.
- Use photos and graphics that support the text.
- Use fancy type, colors, or borders within the text to catch the reader's eye.
- Use hypertext links, if they add to the content.

Brochures are usually designed as an 8- by 11-inch trifold (see Figure 5.3). Plan out the navigational tools and keep them consistent from section to section so the brochure is easy to read. The brochures can be published using a .pdf or .HTML format, but the same advantages and disadvantages discussed in publishing newsletters apply to brochures.

Display the brochures on a prominent place on your home page by placing the link on the index page. You want the teachers and students to be able to easily locate the information; otherwise, it might get lost.

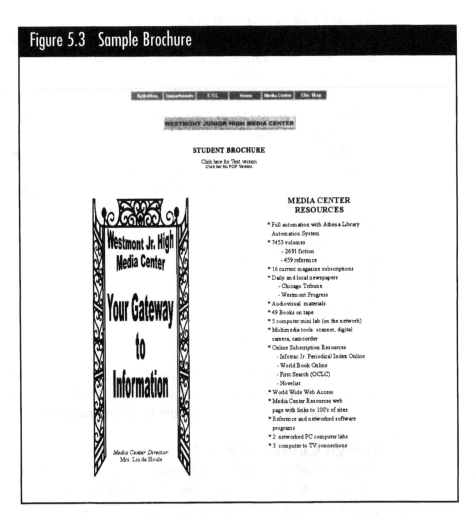

Figure 5.3 Sample Brochure

Westmont Junior High Media Center in Westmont, Illinois

Examples of Brochures
Westmont Junior High School Media Center in Westmont, Illinois
<http://www.westmont.dupage.k12.il.us/jrhigh/MC/MC_brochure.html>
Palm Valley and Rancho Santa Fe Schools Media Center in Phoenix, Arizona
<http://www.lesd.k12.az.us/PV/specials/media/index.html>

Promoting the Brochures
Each time you post a new brochure to your home page, e-mail teachers and administrators. Be sure to include some information about the brochure in the e-mail. Whenever teachers and students have a question about information that is explained in one of your brochures, always refer them to your home page.

Statistical Information and Reports

Media specialists are notorious for compiling statistics and writing reports. It is a time-tested strategy to keep administrators and the school board apprised of what is happening in the library and to demonstrate that the library makes a difference in students' academic achievement. If you really want to toot your library's horn, gather those statistics and reports and post them online for teachers, administrators, and the community to read.

Content of the Statistical Information and Reports Page
You want to illustrate in concrete terms how the library's program contributes to the school's goals and academic achievement. Use facts and figures, but also include descriptions of programs, accomplishments and testimonials from students, teachers, and staff. Update this section of your home page frequently; you want to get the word out at least once a month.

The following are examples of statistical information to include on your home page.

■ Monthly Activities Reports can highlight the instructional role of the library program, including cooperatively planned lessons, inservice training for teachers, and professional development activities.

■ Annual Reports are an opportunity to demonstrate all that the library has done to contribute to the school's success throughout the year, and are a tool that lets your library program shine. The report should include issues that need administrative support such as funding or technology.

■ Library Statistics Reports list the number of classes taught, students using the library during the day and after school, Internet and online database use, circulation statistics, and online reference requests.

■ A Monthly Report includes the name of the teacher, a title and description of the lesson, and information literacy skills taught.

■ Late Breaking News might include information on new online databases, new services, new books, and special events in the library such as Read Across America or National Library Week.

Design Considerations for the Statistical Information and Reports Page

Since you already gather the statistical information for your print reports, posting them to your home page will not be too time consuming. All you have to do is import the information into your Web-authoring program.

The information should be displayed prominently on your home page. Use a catchy title for the link such as How We're Doing, Facts and Figures or Read On. This will entice the reader to click on the hyperlink and discover exactly what the title means. These statistical links should be organized into a user-friendly format using a list or table with headings that indicate the content; for example, monthly report, late breaking news, media center statistics, or new arrivals (see Figure 5.4).

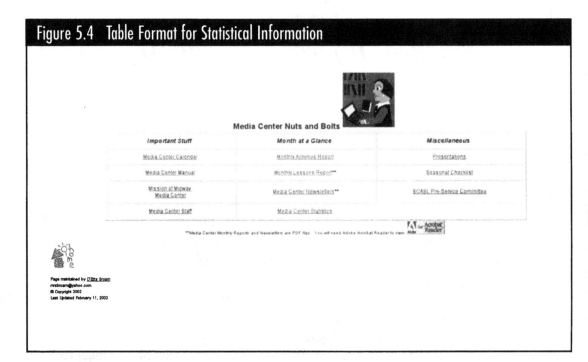

Figure 5.4   Table Format for Statistical Information

Midway Elementary School Media Center in Lexington, South Carolina

As with other sections of your home page, maintain a consistent format and include navigation tools that will return the user to the content table and the index of your home page.

Examples of Statistical Information and Reports Pages

Midway Elementary School Media Center in Lexington, South Carolina
<http://www.lexington1.net/mes/lmc/>
Episcopal High School Library in Jacksonville, Florida
<http://episcopalhigh.org/academics/library/index.htm>
Esperanza Library/Media Center in Phoenix, Arizona
<http://www.lyrene,k12.az.us/schools/Esperanza media/hhenle.htm>

Promoting the Statistical Information and Reports Page

Each time you revise this section of your home page e-mail the principal, teachers, central administration, and board members of your updates.

Online Forms

Give students, teachers, parents, and administrators a voice in library policy and procedures by regularly asking them for their opinions on everything from the curriculum to library services to suggestions for new materials. It is a proactive approach to customer satisfaction and it can be done online by posting surveys, recommendation forms, and a suggestion box to your library's home page.

You probably have evaluation surveys that you distribute each year to students and teachers that you can use on your home page. If you want to update the surveys before posting them to your home page, there are some excellent books on evaluating school libraries that include a variety of surveys. Adapt these to your own library and check with the publisher for copyright approval. Since you have evaluation surveys already in place, it should not take very much time to convert them into Web-based documents. In fact, distributing the survey on your home page will save you time since you will no longer have to copy and collate the forms and put them in teachers' mailboxes.

There are two ways to ensure a high response rate for the surveys. Include a response mechanism with the survey, which could be as simple as entering the names of those that respond in a contest to win a prize. Make the surveys part of the instructional process by building in time at the end of the research process for the students and teachers to complete the survey.

Another way to involve students and teachers in library policy and procedures is to use an online suggestion box. Although many of the ideas may be impossible to implement, you will get some ideas that can help make the library a friendlier place. When implementing a suggestion, be sure to give credit to the student or teacher for the idea; it will go a long way in creating goodwill for your library.

Finally, everyone likes to give their opinion and students and teachers are no exception. You can ask for their input in ordering books, magazines, videos, and CDs by using an online recommendation form.

Design Considerations for Online Forms

You don't have to take a course on designing forms as most Web-authoring programs include forms and there are many sites on the Internet, such as the following, to obtain free form makers.

Forms Site
<http://www.formsite.com>
Free Online Surveys
<http://www.freeonlinesurveys.com/>

In designing the forms, keep them simple and well organized. Provide directions for each area of the form. These directions are usually placed above or to the left of the form box or a combination of both (see Figure 5.5).

There are several features that should be placed on your online forms. Submit and clear buttons should be part of the form and are placed at the bottom of the form. Provide space for the person's name and e-mail address; this will ensure that the survey or recommendation is treated seriously. Finally, include navigation tools that will return the user to the index of your home page.

As with other sections of your home page, maintain a consistent format. Use the same colors, fonts, and placement of navigation tools.

Figure 5.5   Location of Questions on Forms

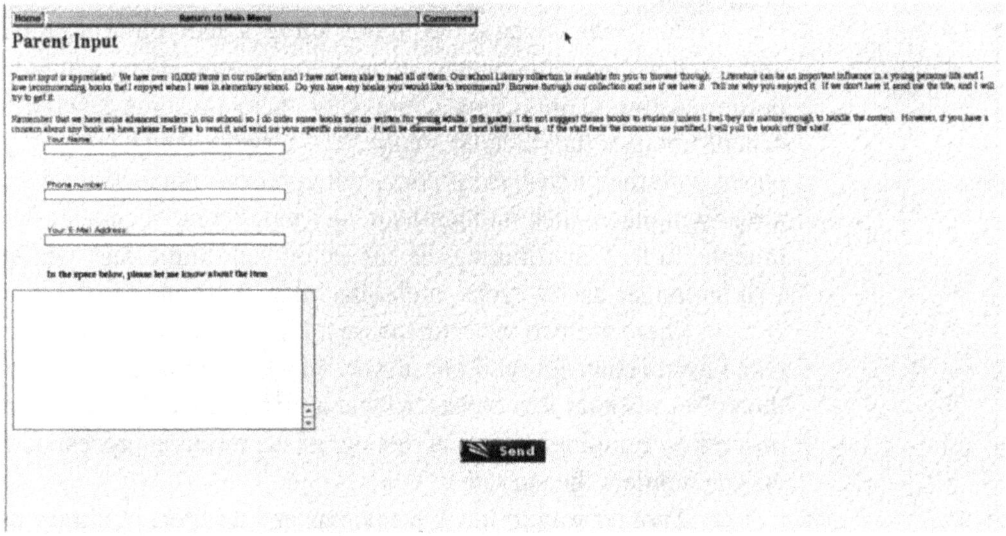

Mt. Erie Elementary School Library in Anacortes, Washington

Examples of Online Forms

Jasper Elementary School Media Center in Chapel Hill, North Carolina
<http://www.ils.unc.edu/~webbj/inls181/eval.html>
Birch Lane Elementary School Library in Davis, California
<http://www.birchlane.davis.ca.us/library/Default.htm>
Bessie Chin High School Library in Redwood, California
<http://rhsweb.org/library/index.html>
Mt. Erie Elementary School Library in Anacortes, Washington
<http://mte.asd103.org/library/library.htm>
Archbishop Ryan High School in Philadelphia, Pennsylvania
<http://www.ryanhs.org/library/teacher/libform.html>

Promoting the Online Forms

Incorporate the evaluation of your information skills program as part of your instructional units. Students and teachers complete the evaluation forms on their last day in the library. Each time you teach a class, mention there is a suggestion box on the home page and ask the students to complete these forms. When you get your budget allocation, e-mail teachers and ask them to assist you in ordering materials by completing the suggestion survey on your home page. Be sure to include the address of the home page in the e-mail.

Library Logo

Nike has its swoosh, ALA has *@your library*, and your library should also have its own logo or graphic identity. It is another way to visually promote your library and tell its story. The logo becomes a symbol for the library. It is a strategic marketing tool that communicates your library's mission and services. You can use your logo on your home page and on all library promotional material.

Ideally, your logo's design is a personal symbol for your library's mission and services. You don't have to be an artist to create your library's logo. Involve your students through a library logo contest. Advertise the logo contest on your home page, on your library's bulletin boards, and in art and graphic design classes. Schedule a meeting with interested students to explain the purpose of the logo, discuss logo formats and designs, outline the selection process, and provide samples of logos from other school libraries.

Design Considerations for Library Logos

Your logo should grab the attention of your teachers, administrators, and students, but the design should be simple so the message conveyed in the logo is remembered. There are four types of designs for logos: those made up of images; logos that use only letters; those that use words; and finally logos that mix images, letters, and words.

Once you choose the form of the logo, you will have to focus on several other design issues. Make sure the type is at least 10 point, but no larger than 14 point and the colors in your logo are consistent with colors on your home page. Save the file as a .jpeg or .gif if your logo design includes images. You can combine an image with text by using a program like PhotoShop or Paint. Again the file must be saved as a .jpeg or .gif with a resolution of 72 pixels per inch. This resolution guarantees that the logo will be not be fuzzy. You can also use clip art in your logo, but remember to follow all copyright laws. Don't use an animated logo; though it may look cute, it will take too long to load. The placement of the logo should be consistent from page to page; logos are usually found in the center or in the upper left-hand corner of the home page. If all of this seems like just too much work, don't be discouraged, ALA has come to your rescue. ALA has logos that you can use on your home page (see Figure 5.6).

This logo is downloadable at ALA's Web site:
<http://cs.ala.org/@yourlibrary/download1.cfm>

Figure 5.6   ALA Logo

Examples of School Library Logos

West Junior High Library Media Center in Pittsburgh, Pennsylvania
<http://www.whsd.k12.pa.us/wj/mediacenter1/index.html>
Greenway Media Center in Beaverton, Oregon
<http://www.beavton.k12.or.us/greenway/media/grnwymedia.html>
Jefferson Elementary School Media Center in Chapel Hill, North Carolina
<http://www.ils.unc.edu/~webbj/inls181/jasper.html#Home>
Thayer Middle School Library in Thayer, Missouri
<http://thayer.k12.mo.us/library/library.htm>
Penn High Library Media Center in Palos Verdes Estates, California
<http://www.pvpusd.k12.ca.us/pvphs/top.html>

Promoting the Library Logo

There are a number of ways that you can advertise your logo. Make the library logo the lead story in one of your newsletters and explain the logo's design, meaning, and use. If you held a contest to design the logo, create a bulletin board displaying the logo along with the names and photos of students who participated in the contest. In addition, have your principal announce the name of the student who designed the winning logo and don't forget to e-mail the logo to teachers and administrators.

Virtual Bulletin Board Displays

Bulletin board displays make the library attractive and continually create interest for its programs and services among students and staff. If a picture is worth a thousand words, then a bulletin board display of photos sharing what the library does every day is worth a million words. Bulletin board displays are an important tool in educating teachers and administrators that the library is critical to student success.

Now, imagine the impact of a virtual bulletin board display on your library's home page. Parents, the school board, and members of the community will see the services and programs in the library that are having a positive impact on student learning. Virtual bulletin board displays will make a difference in getting the word out and promoting your library program.

Planning Virtual Bulletin Board Displays

As with any new project, creating a virtual bulletin board display will require additional time, but once you've created the home page, you can save the layout so it can be used each year. All you will have to do is change the pictures. So, virtual bulletin board displays won't be as time consuming as you think.

Virtual bulletin board displays should be changed frequently, as with other library displays. Displays should be posted for at least two weeks, but no longer than a month; you want to continually arouse interest and have students, teachers, administrators, and the community coming back to your home page to see what is happening in the library.

Keep a digital camera handy because you don't want to miss a photo opportunity. Use action shots of students and teachers engaged in learning activities. Students enjoy looking at pictures of their classmates and this will keep them coming back to the library's home page to see what new pictures have been posted. Remember to follow your district's guidelines regarding publishing photos of students on the Internet.

If students help you decorate your library's bulletin boards, they can also assist with the virtual bulletin board displays by designing graphics to incorporate into the displays. There are several ways that you can involve students. If you have a student advisory board or student assistants, make the virtual bulletin board displays one of their yearly projects. You could also make this a collaborative project working with the computer, art, and graphic arts teachers. They could have their students design graphics for the virtual bulletin board displays as part of a class project.

Content of Virtual Bulletin Board Displays

Virtual bulletin board displays should promote student learning and highlight the instructional role of the library. Be sure to include captions that describe each activity and its purpose. The content is similar to the themes that you use on the library's bulletin boards and includes the following:

- Research Assignments—These displays feature students using the library and displays of completed research projects. Virtual bulletin boards are a powerful motivational tool in student learning because students are given an opportunity to share their work with a worldwide audience.
- Reading Promotion—Use photos of teachers and students sharing their favorite books, author visits, virtual book reviews, book displays, Read Across America, and Teen Read Week.
- Special Events—Create online displays of special events programming.
- Library Orientation—In September, post pictures of students participating in the library's orientation; gather comments from students and teachers to include as captions to the photos.
- Holidays and Seasons—Post displays of holiday projects that were researched and created in the library.
- Library Resources—Displays of students using the Internet, online databases, and reference resources.

Design Considerations for Virtual Bulletin Board Displays

As with other sections of your home page, the virtual bulletin board displays should be visually pleasing. Backgrounds should be kept simple because the focus is on the display. Use headlines and captions that are eye-catching to describe the activity. Vary the colors and fonts of the captions, but don't make them look too busy.

Since you will be using a mix of pictures and graphics in your display, keep the files small; you don't want the page to take too long to load. Also, save all picture files as .jpegs or .gifs.

The least complicated design for the virtual bulletin board is a table. With this format, you can insert your pictures in each cell and then place the captions under, over, or through each picture. Next, create a category on the index of your home page for your virtual bulletin board displays. Choose a title, such as Library Photo Galley or Library Photo Album that will immediately let the viewer know what they are going to see.

Be sure to include navigational tools that will return the user to the index of your home page.

Examples of Virtual Bulletin Board Displays

Midway Media Center in Lexington, Kentucky
<http://www.lex1.k12.state.sc.us/mes/lmc/photos.html>
Athens Academy Media Center in Athens, Georgia
<http://www.athensacademy.org/instruct/centers/ls_media/happening.html>

Promoting Virtual Bulletin Board Displays

E-mail teachers whenever they and their students are part of a virtual bulletin board display and watch what happens when word of mouth takes over.

Contests

Everyone enjoys a contest. Library contests generate enthusiasm among teachers and students and promote the library as an exciting place. Your home page provides an opportunity to use contests as online promotions for your library's services and resources. Creating your own Web-based contests is quite similar to what you already do, but with an added bonus. The contests will reach a wider audience and will promote the role that your library plays in the school's curriculum.

Content of Contests

The source of inspiration for your library contests is everywhere from trivia to riddles to reading. The contests can be tied to your special events programming, seasonal and national holidays, reading promotion, and activities in the school.

Planning Contests

Creating your own Web-based contests is quite similar to what you already do and won't take very much time; in fact, many of the contests that you already use can easily become online contests. Begin planning your contests in September; post a new contest every three to four weeks on your home page to continually generate excitement for your library.

Decide the purpose of the contests—some contests are part of your special events programming while others can be used to create interest in the library. Keep the contest rules simple and include them on your home page.

If you are going to award prizes, you will have to solicit local businesses. This should be done at the end of the school year since you will begin your contests in September. Recognize these businesses on your home page by including their names and the prizes donated next to the names of the contest winners. Be sure to follow your district's guidelines for publishing students' names on the Internet.

Design Considerations for Contests

Display the link for the contests in a prominent place on your home page; you want to encourage as much participation as possible (see Figure 5.7). If you are using a fill-in-the-blanks form, most Web-authoring programs include form makers or you can use free form makers found on Internet sites such as freeforms.com.

Just as you would decorate a display or bulletin board for your contests, do the same with your contest pages. Use colorful backgrounds and graphics that relate to the contest's theme. As with other sections of your home page, include navigational tools to direct the user back to the index of your home page.

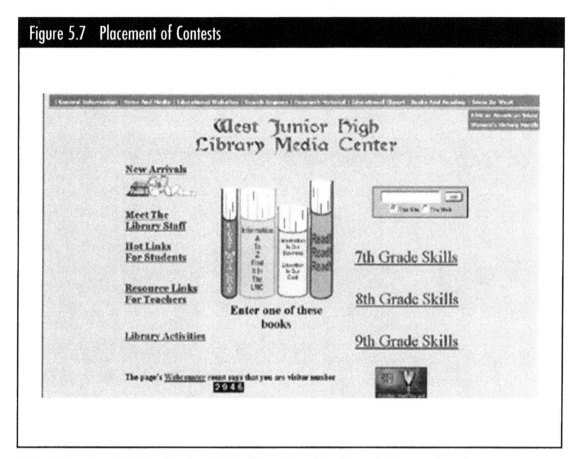

Figure 5.7 Placement of Contests

West Woodland Hills Junior High School in Pittsburgh, Pennsylvania

Examples of Contests
Roseman Elementary School Library in Rosman, North Carolina
<http://www.transylvania.k12.nc.us/schools/res/media/contest2.html>
New Palestine Elementary School Media Center in New Palestine, Indiana
<http://npe.newpal.k12.in.us/nlwwinners.html>
West Junior High School Media Center in Pittsburgh, Pennsylvania
<http://www.whsd.k12.pa.us/wj/mediacenter1/index.html>

Promoting Contests
Use your school's daily announcements to herald the beginning of each contest. Post signs in the library alerting students to the contests. Finally, at the first faculty meeting, give teachers a schedule of the year's library contests and use e-mail to remind them to tell their students about the contests.

6

Special Events

Introduction

Special events create excitement and anticipation and are an opportunity to demonstrate to students, teachers, parents, and the community that libraries are not only repositories of knowledge and information, but also places where enjoyable programs occur. Read Across America, National Library Week, Multicultural Week, Spelling and Geography Bees, and national and seasonal holiday celebrations are times to shine the spotlight on your library by offering special programs to celebrate these occasions. School librarians use special events to make the library an exciting place for students and staff. Orchestrating these activities and programs is a time-consuming task, but the benefits far outweigh the effort. Some of the benefits are increased visibility for the library and its services and resources; promotion of lifelong learning; enrichment for students and teachers, and increased opportunities for collaboration with teachers and community members. These special events generate such positive feelings and outcomes that it seems a shame they have to end. But they don't have to, because participants, as well as those who were not able to attend, can relive them virtually on the library's home page.

Planning Special Events

Organizing successful special events requires several steps. The first of these is to determine your audience. Target many groups—students, teachers, parents, and the community—but tailor each event to a specific audience. Next, set your goals. What do you hope to accomplish as a result of these activities? When the audience and goals have been established, come up with creative ideas to determine the type of activities and programs that you will sponsor in your library. You can do this by forming a committee of students, teachers, parents, and community members to provide input, or by designing an interest survey that is distributed to teachers, parents, and students. Both methods will help you discover the type of programs that will be most popular in your library. Keep in mind that posting these events to your home page is going to extend the time frame for each, so set up a timetable for each special event and allow for that in your planning.

NetFirst Calendar from the Online Computer Library Center (OCLC) <http:www.oclc.org/oclc/menu/netcalendar.htm> is a useful tool for special event planning as it lists holidays, events, activities, and resources three months in advance.

Focus your events around holidays, themes, school subjects, and the students' grade levels. Evaluate what you've done through observation or surveys or a combination of both. Evaluation is important because it provides feedback on the reasons for the program's success or items that need to be changed (see Figure 6.1). Make it easy for your teachers to complete the evaluation form by locating it with each special event on your calendar. With collaboration from all segments of the community, these special events will encourage wider participation and showcase your library and its programs.

Content of Special Events

The content of the special events that you present in your library is designed for enrichment, entertainment, and curriculum support, while at the same time meant to create an air of celebration. Here are some ideas that you can use for displaying your special events on your home page.

Special Events Calendar

Entice teachers and students to your special events programming by posting a calendar on the special events section of your home page. This calendar lists each month's events, the dates, the times, and the activities. Decorate the calendar with graphics that illustrate each event. Create a promotional logo that students and teachers will associate with your special events. Sponsor a logo contest involving the entire school by advertising it on your school's morning announcements, on your home page, and bulletin boards. Post the name of the student who designed the winning special events' logo on your home page. Include your e-mail address and phone number on the calendar so people with questions about an event can contact you.

Design Considerations for the Special Events Calendar

The special events calendar is posted to the special events section of your home page and becomes the informational link to all special events. Format the special events calendar as a list or a table. You can also arrange the calendar as a two-column table with the first column listing the date and the second column listing the event. The months are displayed at the top of the calendar (see Figure 6.2). Displaying your special events calendar as a table has the advantage of looking like an actual calendar with graphics and photos of the events. Alternatively you can display all the events for the month or year on the calendar using photos and graphics (see Figure 6.3). Just a reminder—save all pictures and graphics in a .jpeg or .gif format. These links should be arranged directly below the current month's calendar. Display the logo for your special events calendar at the top of the page. Remember to include navigational tools so the users can get back to the index of your home page.

Figure 6.1   Special Event Evaluation Form

Special Event Evaluation Form

Your Name

Name of the Event

We hope you enjoyed the program that you attended in the library and would like you to share your thoughts on the program with us by completing this survey.
Thank you for your help.

The program held the students' attention.
  ◉ Yes   ◉ No

The program met your expectations.
  ◉ Yes   ◉ No

List the program's strengths.

List the program's weaknesses.

Would you recommend this program for next year? Explain your answer.

SUBMIT   CLEAR

Figure 6.2 Table Format

What's Happening @ Midway Elementary Media Center?
2001 - 2002

August-October	November-February	March-May	Summer
October 29, 2001	MES faculty and staff meet and discuss _Sullivan's Island: A Low Country Tale_ by Dorothea Benton Frank		
November 8, 2001	4th Grade Book Club discusses _Jackie and Me_ by Dan Gutman and _A Letter to Mrs. Roosevelt_ by C. Coco DeYoung		
November 13-17, 2001 _National Children's Book Week_	Author Heidi E. Y. Stemple Visits Grades 1-4 • Click here to take the quiz! • See pictures of Mrs. Stemple's visit!		
December 3-7, 2001	Aardvark Week		
December 12, 2001	Mr. Thompson reads stories about Curious George to Mrs. Roberson and Mrs. Davis' first grades!		
January 28-February 8, 2002	Book Fair		

Midway Elementary School Media Center in Lexington, South Carolina

Examples of Special Events Calendars

Midway Elementary Media Center in Lexington, South Carolina
<http://www.lexington1.net/mes/lmc/info.html>
Hilltop Primary School Media Center in Mound, Minnesota
<http://www.westonka.k12.mn.us/hilltop/teachers/olaussen%20web/olaussenindex.html>
Jones Elementary Media Center in Atlanta, Georgia
<http://www.arches.uga.edu/~gregoryo/mediacentercalendar.htm>
Islip Terrace Junior High School Media Center in Islip Terrace, New York
<http://www.eastislip.k12.ny.us/itjhs/Ellen/calendar.html>
Geebung State School Library in Brisbane, Queensland, Australia
<http://www.geebungss.qld.edu.au/glib.htm>
White Knoll High School Media Center in Lexington, South Carolina
<http://www.lexington1.net/lv/wkhs/hp.nsf/HomePages/wkhmedia>
Maple Shade Elementary Media Center in Maple Shade, New Jersey
<http://www.geocities.com/readmebook/>
Springbrook High School in Rockville, Maryland
<http://www.mcps.k12.md.us/schools/springbrookhs/media.html>
San Lorenzo Valley Elementary School in Felton, California
<http://www.sle.slv.k12.ca.us/~skeil/>

Promoting the Special Events Calendar

At the start of the school year, notify teachers that a listing of the year's special events can be found on your home page on the special events calendar. Follow this up with e-mail alerting them to check the calendar for updates. Request that a blurb about your special events be read as part of the morning announcements and ask the principal to include this promotional information in the monthly newsletter. Expand this awareness to the public library by asking them to include a link to your special events calendar on their home page. Reciprocate by posting the public library's special events on your calendar.

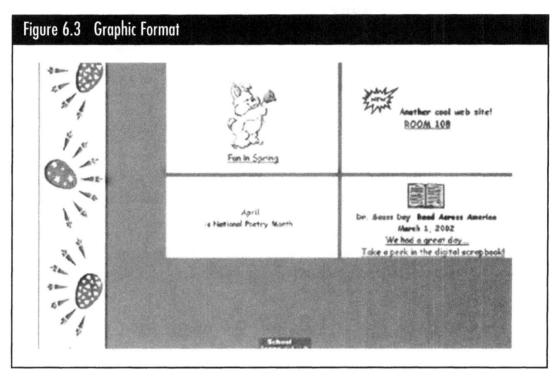

Figure 6.3 Graphic Format

Hilltop Primary School Media Center in Mound, Minnesota

Read Across America

Every year libraries commemorate Dr. Seuss as part of Read Across America celebrations. These celebrations involve administrators, teachers, students, and parents and culminate in programs and activities designed to foster a love of reading. Promote your library by including Read Across America festivities on the special events section of your library home page.

Content of Read Across America

There are many activities that take place during Read Across America that you can include on your home page.

- Set up an interview session with your student library assistants and your principal. The following is a sample question for the students to ask the principal: "What is your favorite book and how did it influence your life? What is the importance of reading?"
- Have the students from your school's television studio course videotape the interview and convert the video into a Web-based format so it can be posted on your special events page.

- As an alternative to a face-to-face interview, ask your principal to write a blurb on the most influential book in his or her life and post a photo of the principal holding the book along with the blurb on your home page.
- Photograph your teachers and students reading their favorite books.
- Create an e-mail link on your home page called Read Across America and ask students and parents to send you the titles and authors of their favorite books. They can also write a book review, which can be included on the Read Across America page for all to view.
- Design a calendar, which includes a biography of authors and illustrators and also shows their names and birthdays. Invite students to see if they share a birthday with an author or illustrator. When they click on the author's name the link takes them to a biography of the author or illustrator and their work. List the authors and illustrators' books that are available in your library and invite students to read them and submit a book review that can be posted on your home page.
- Invite a celebrity to read a book in your library. Videotape the session or use your digital camera and capture photos of the session and post them on your home page.
- Solicit testimonials from parents and teachers about the impact of reading on their lives.
- Photograph the activities that are taking place in your library during Read Across America Week and create virtual bulletin board displays. Describe each activity and include photos with captions along with students' comments.
- This is also a good time to involve the community by inviting parents to join in the festivities, such as a pajama party where bedtime stories are read to children. This provides another photo opportunity to enhance your home page.

Planning Read Across America

E-mail the principal and teachers to invite them to participate in the library's Read Across America activities and ask them to pose for a digital photo with their favorite book. Make it easy for all involved by bringing the book with you when you take their photos.

If your students are going to interview the principal, schedule a meeting of the students and review the interview format with them. Give the principal plenty of advance notice and copies of the interview questions.

Testimonials on reading can be gathered from students and teachers whenever they visit the library and then posted on your home page.

Design Considerations for Read Across America

Place a colorful banner advertising the Read Across America page on the index of your home page. Read Across America activities can be accessed through the special events calendar and on the index of your home page. Your list of events can be made visually attractive by using a photograph or graphic with the name of the event and its description. Make this page exciting by using different colors and design elements. Don't forget that ALA and NEA have many graphics that can be used for this section of your home page.

When publishing photos of students on your home page, follow your district's policies. Always use a .jpeg and .gif format for photos and graphics. If you are including a video of the Read Across America activities, post links to Internet sites, such as the following, where free viewers can be downloaded.

QuickTime Pro
    <http://www.apple.com/quicktime/>
Multimedia Xplorer
    <http://www.moonsoftware.com/>
MPEG Player
    <http://www.mpeg.org/MPEG/MSSG/>

If community businesses have helped in the celebration by contributing prizes, make sure you acknowledge them on your home page.

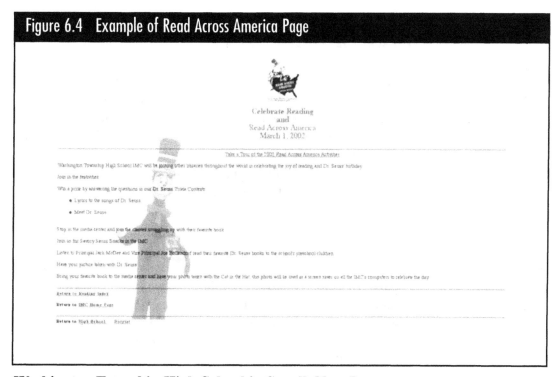

Figure 6.4   Example of Read Across America Page

Washington Township High School in Sewell, New Jersey

Examples of Read Across America Pages
Washington Township High School Media Center in Sewell, New Jersey
    <http://www.wtps.org/wths/imc/index.html>
Delsea Regional High School in Franklinville, New Jersey
    <http://www.delsea.k12.nj.us/Academic/MediaCenter/hs/main.htm>
Burroughs-Molette Elementary Media Center in Brunswick, Georgia
    <http://www.glynn.k12.ga.us/~jhamlin/mc/raa.html>
Maple Shade Elementary Media Center in Maple Shade, New Jersey
    <http://www.geocities.com/readmebook/>
The Elkins Park School Library in Elkins Park, Pennsylvania
    <http://mciu.org/~epsweb/library.htm>
Greensfarms Elementary Academy in Westport, Connecticut
    <http://www.gfacademy.org/community/Departments/Library/
    gfalibrary.html>

Promoting Read Across America

This is a national event and is heavily publicized by local television and radio stations. Take the lead from them and create your own media blitz for this special event. Dress your student library assistants in *Cat in the Hat* costumes and hats and have them publicize Read Across America events as part of the morning announcements.

Write a column for your principal's monthly newsletter notifying parents that they can receive information on Read Across America activities on the special events section of your home page. E-mail teachers to inform them of each day's events. Alert your district's public relations director as well as local newspapers and television stations of your planned activities so these can be advertised.

National Library Week

This is a time to celebrate libraries and librarians and all they do for their communities. It is a time to advertise the library as an indispensable resource in children's lives. Publicize the fact that libraries are more than storehouses for books; they are community centers that connect students, teachers, parents, and administrators to valuable services and resources. During National Library Week, school libraries sponsor exciting programs ranging from family night at the library to book fairs. The goal of these activities is to promote the school library. Now you can extend these festivities by posting National Library Week activities to your home page.

Content of National Library Week

- Use ALA's promotional logo @ Your Library on your National Library Week Events page. Be sure to include their fact sheets about libraries as well as your library's daily and monthly statistics. This statistical information should include student and class use of the library, circulation statistics, Internet and online database use, classes taught, and special projects that were completed in your school library. These facts publicize all that your library does to promote student learning.
- Ask students to design a contest about your library. Use an interactive form on your National Library Week page and ask questions about the number of books in the library, the date when the library was built, the name of the oldest book, the name of the first librarian, hours of operation—the list of questions is endless.
- Sponsor a bookmark or book cover design contest highlighting National Library Week and post the winning designs on your home page.
- Encourage parents to take a virtual tour of the library. After they have completed the tour, ask them to sign the virtual guest book that will enter them in a drawing for a prize.
- Create virtual bulletin board displays of the activities during National Library Week.
- Describe each activity and include captions to illustrate each photo exhibit.
- Collect testimonials from students, teachers, parents, and administrators about the influence of libraries and librarians on their lives.
- Invite your principal to formally introduce National Library Week by writing and reading a proclamation to the students.
- Display a photograph of you and the principal with the proclamation on the special events page.

Planning National Library Week

As with other special events, planning begins early. Let the principal know in September that you would like him or her to write a proclamation about the school library's influence on learning. E-mail a sample of ALA's proclamation for National Library Week to use as a model. Also include a copy of the *Colorado Study*, ALA statistics, as well as your own library statistics, which can be utilized in the proclamation about libraries and academic achievement.

National Library Week provides myriad opportunities for collaboration with teachers. Target language arts teachers at each grade level and ask them to give a homework assignment that asks students to write about libraries. E-mail teachers to ask them to describe the influence of libraries on their lives; excerpts from these responses can be used as testimonials. Collaborate with the graphic arts and art teachers and have their students participate in book cover and bookmark design contests. Since the winning designs must be completed before National Library Week, meet with teachers at the beginning of the second semester to discuss your ideas and get their input about the design contests. Visit their classes and discuss the contest with the students. Use this as an opportunity to inform them about National Library Week and their role in it.

If you are going to sponsor contests and award prizes, solicit businesses for donations. As an incentive for the business, post a photo of a representative from the business giving the prize to the winning students on your home page. Mention the names of the businesses that donated the prizes for the contests in your promotional material as well as on your home page. Remember to follow your district's policy regarding publishing students' names on the Internet.

Design Considerations for National Library Week

Use a colorful banner on the index of your home page as a reminder to parents, students, teachers, and administrators of this special event. National Library Week activities are accessed from your special events calendar. Simply create a link using the words National Library Week. Include the purpose of National Library Week and links to each activity on this page. As with the other special events pages, make this page visually exciting by using vibrant colors, photographs, and varying fonts. After all, this page is a celebration of libraries.

Scan the winning bookmark or book cover designs to use on your National Library Week page. Use a program like PhotoShop or Paint to convert the pictures into a .jpeg or .gif format. The file must be saved with a resolution of 72 pixels per inch. This resolution guarantees that the graphic will be not be fuzzy. As with all photos that you use on this page, keep the file size small.

Don't forget to include navigational tools, as you want the user to easily locate the special events page and the index of your home page.

Examples of National Library Week Pages

Midway Elementary School in Lexington, South Carolina
<http://www.lexington1.net/mes/lmc/programs.html#National Library/TV Turnoff Week>
New Palestine Elementary School in New Palestine, Indiana
<http://npe.newpal.k12.in.us/nlwwinners.html>

The Edna M. Fielder Elementary School in Katy, Texas
<http://www.katy.isd.tenet.edu/fe/library/fielderlibrary/fielderlibrary.html>

Promoting National Library Week

Ask the principal to read the National Library Week proclamation as the only announcement at the start of the week. Include the proclamation in the principal's monthly newsletter and in the notice that National Library Week events can be accessed through the library's home page. Don't forget to include the library's URL. Use your school's morning announcements to publicize each day's activities and winners of any contests that you sponsor. Finally, e-mail teachers to remind them of each day's events.

Holiday Celebrations

Holiday celebrations present opportunities to generate enthusiasm among students, cooperatively plan activities with teachers, and promote your library at the same time. You can do this by building resource-based units around national, local, seasonal, and ethnic holiday celebrations. The activities for these celebrations are ideal for posting on your home page.

Content of the Holiday Celebrations Page

Holidays provide a continual source of themes for your home page. The ideas suggested here can be applied to all the holidays on your special events calendar.

- Sponsor creative writing contests where students write poetry or short stories based on holiday themes. Work with the language arts and foreign language teachers to design these contests. The best short stories and poems are posted to the holiday celebration section of your special events page with the student's first name and picture.
- Create a holiday recipe exchange. Students and their parents can submit recipes by completing an online form on your holiday page. You don't have to get all of the holiday recipes at once. Keep the online holiday submission form on your page and as your receive each recipe, organize them by holiday to use from year to year.
- Collaborate with the art and graphic arts teachers to sponsor a holiday craft and greeting card design contest. The winning designs are posted to the holiday celebration page.
- Work with the social studies teachers to create multimedia presentations of national and international holidays and post the best of these presentations on your holiday celebration page.
- Post a holiday trivia contest on your holiday celebration page. Students use an online form to submit their answers. Winners of the trivia contest are entered into a drawing for a prize from a local bookstore.
- Create a virtual bulletin board of holiday celebrations. For example, photograph the elementary school students in their Halloween costumes with their favorite Halloween book. This idea can be used for most holiday celebrations.

Planning the Holiday Celebrations Page

Contact teachers in September and arrange to meet with them in person or via e-mail to collaboratively plan these holiday celebrations. Since there are so many holidays throughout the year, ask the teachers which holidays they would like to use as resource-based units and cooperatively design the activities including the goals and objectives, resources, responsibilities, assessment, and a rubric for grading.

Determine the starting and ending dates for any contests and post them on your holiday celebrations page. At the beginning of the school year, contact local businesses and ask them to donate prizes as awards for the contests. Remember to acknowledge their contributions next to the names of the contest winners and follow your district's guidelines in posting names of students on your home page.

If you are planning a holiday trivia contest, design the trivia questions yourself or use trivia sites on the Internet. The following are sites that provide trivia questions.

The Trivial Portal
      <http://www.funtrivia.com/>
Useless Knowledge
      <http://thinks.com/puzzles/lit-trivia.htm>
Literary Trivia
      <http://thinks.com/puzzles/lit-trivia.htm>
For a holiday listing by month visit
      <http://www.holidays.net/dates.htm>
E-mail Reminders: Submit your e-mail address and ask to be added to their mailing list. You will then receive e-mails reminding you about all upcoming holidays.
      <http://www.melizo.com/holidays/hol_list.htm>

Design Considerations for the Holiday Celebrations Page

Your holiday page is accessed through your special events calendar. Use text or a graphic on the calendar to represent the specific holiday; this will become the link to that month's holiday activities. As with the other sections of your special events page, make the holiday page visually attractive by using graphics, colors, and varying fonts.

Since you are sponsoring online contests, posting testimonials, and acquiring holiday recipes, you will have to design forms for each of these. Your Web-authoring program has a form maker or you can use the following Internet sites.

Form Creators
      <http://www.forms.com>
      <http://www.wiscforms.com>

If using student artwork, scan it into a program like PhotoShop or Paint to convert the pictures into a format that you can use on your home page. Save the pictures as a .jpeg or .gif. The file must be saved with a resolution of 72 pixels per inch so the graphics are not fuzzy. As with any graphics used on your home page, remember to keep the file size small so that your page will load quickly.

The holiday multimedia presentations must be converted into an .HTML format. This is very easy to do with most programs such as PowerPoint; just save it as an .HTML file so that it can be posted to your holiday celebrations page. Though it will not have the interactivity of the original presentation, it will allow other students in the school, parents, and the worldwide community to see the holiday projects created by students through research in your library. As with all of your special events, include navigation links back to the special events calendar and the index of your home page.

Example of a Holiday Celebrations Page

MLS Media Center in Winnsboro, South Carolina
<http://www.myschoolonline.com/page/0,1871,45665-140806-48-7601,00.html>

Promoting the Holiday Celebrations Page

Posting student projects, writing, or artwork on your home page creates a buzz among students, which becomes the best form of advertisement. E-mail teachers every time you add a new event to your special events calendar. Teachers who collaborated on special events projects will look forward to seeing their students' projects on your home page, so remember to e-mail them as soon as the projects are posted to the home page. Ask them to send a letter home with the students so parents can view their children's projects as well. This promotes the work of teachers and the library and at the same time gives pleasure to parents.

Guest Speakers

Guest speakers can span the entire alphabet from A to Z—from authors to zoos. As they share their expertise with students, they inspire and engage students, extend the collaborative process, enrich and support the curriculum, and promote your library program. Students and teachers delight in coming to the library to listen to guest speakers and participate in demonstrations, but space is often limited and not all students can attend; therefore, your home page becomes the conduit for all the students in your school to enjoy the library's guest speakers. A digital or video camera and a little extra time are all that is needed to display your guest speaker programming on your special events page.

Content of the Guest Speaker Page

The content of the programs is as varied as the themes in your school's curriculum. Your guest speakers can be authors, storytellers, puppeteers, musicians, mobile zoos, world travelers, artists, magicians, and comedians, and they can range from performance artists to volunteers such as parents, teachers, community members, and students.

The following are examples of ways to expand the scope of your guest speaker programming to the entire school.

- Follow the lead of the television and movie industry and give your students a preview of your guest speakers on your home page.
- These previews should include a picture and biography of the speaker and a description of the topic. Use these previews to actively involve students by including interactive forms where students can post questions to the guest speaker.
- Submit these questions to the speaker prior to the visit, so they can be answered during the presentation.

- After the presentation post the speaker's answers to the questions on the guest speaker page.
- Students follow up this activity by creating projects and displays based on the speaker's presentation; post the best projects on the guest speaker page.
- Use comments from the guest speaker evaluation forms as testimonials on your guest speaker page.
- Create virtual bulletin board displays of the presentations using a videotape or photo format.

Planning the Guest Speaker Page

If you are new at organizing guest speaker presentations, there are many books that are helpful in planning this special event from start to finish for your library. It is important to note that the time frame for planning guest speaker programming begins in September and lasts around four to five weeks for each speaker's presentation. Placing this program on your special events page will entail at least an additional week because you will have to design the page, scan photos, and write descriptions and captions.

The key to a successful guest speaker program is planning. This means you and your teachers will have to collaboratively plan the activities that precede and conclude the guest speaker's visit. Since many of the guest speakers' topics will correspond to a curriculum theme, you will have to select the subjects and grade levels of students who attend the event.

Assign the task of videotaping the presentation or taking photographs to a parent volunteer, a student assistant, or a member of your library staff. Meet with the volunteer to discuss exactly what you want them to do and explain the type of camera and video shots you will need for your virtual displays.

Design Considerations for the Guest Speaker Page

As with all the other sections of your special events page, the guest speaker page is accessed from the special events calendar by creating a hyperlink from the calendar to the event. The same design rules used for your other special events apply to your guest speaker page. As a reminder, if you are going to include videotape on the page, be sure to provide links to sites such as QuickTime Pro and MPEG Player, where video viewers can be downloaded. Finally, your navigation tools should get the user back to the special events calendar and the index of your home page.

Example of a Guest Speaker Page

SHS Media Center in Wabash, Indiana
<http://www.msdwc.k12.in.us/shs/Mcnews2.htm>

Promoting the Guest Speaker Page

The promotional efforts for each of your guest speakers should begin at the start of the school year with your back-to-school newsletter and followed up by frequent e-mails. Since guest speaker presentations are a collaborative project, ask teachers to notify parents about the activities for the guest speakers and include the library's URL with the notifications.

Chapter Seven

Reading

Introduction

Wake Up and Read; For a Richer, Fuller Life, Read; Read and Watch Your World Grow, Reading is the Key; Know What You Are Talking About — Read; Explore Inner Space; Reading is What's Happening; Be All You Can Be — Read; Reading is For Everybody; You've Got a Right to Read; Reading Makes the World Go Round; Get Ahead — Read; Grow With Books; A Nation of Readers; Take Time to Read; Kids Who Read Succeed; Read! Learn! Connect! These well-known slogans of National Library Week are testimonials to the importance of reading.

Reading is, of course, beneficial in numerous ways. It is a critical component in academic success; it promotes lifelong learning; it has the power to change people's lives and it opens up a world of imagination where students participate in tales of adventure, romance, and mystery.

Though librarians design activities to promote literacy and the enjoyment of reading, the reality is that students have many demands and distractions in their busy lives such as school, sports, work, television, the Internet, and video games. This has led them to expect quick bytes and to develop a "fast food" mentality for entertainment needs, and unfortunately, reading does not fit that bill. So, how do we entice students into the habit of reading for pleasure? One way is to connect students' love of technology with the joy of reading. This can be done with a home page that combines a pastime that students enjoy—browsing the Internet—with reading promotion. A home page celebrates reading and fosters a community of readers who share their love of reading with others in the school. A home page's interactive and multimedia features make it a perfect vehicle for reading promotion that can engage and excite students.

Electronic Stories

Story writing is an activity that engages students in learning, improves their reading, language and writing skills, and allows them to use their imagination in a creative process. With technology, the process of writing stories is transformed from pen and pencil into multimedia presentations that are shared with the rest of the world via a library's home page.

Content of Electronic Stories

Electronic stories can be picture books, read-along books with audio files, or picture books with music. The content of the stories is as vast as a student's imagination and can include stories created around a theme to translations of classic folk tales.

Planning Electronic Stories

This is another opportunity to cooperatively plan a lesson with teachers. In fact, this is a good example of an interdisciplinary project. You can collaborate with the subject area teachers to create an electronic story crafted around a theme. The time frame for this unit is about three to four weeks. One of the first things to do is delineate the areas of responsibility. For example, the language arts teacher works with the students, assisting them with crafting their stories, while the subject area teacher concentrates on content and the overall appearance of the story. The media specialist's responsibilities include locating resources, both print and electronic, teaching the multimedia software program, and creating the Web page that will house the electronic stories.

A good planning tool for students is a storyboard. This will help the student remain organized and visualize how their stories will be displayed on the Internet.

Design Considerations for Electronic Stories

Create a link for the electronic stories on the reading section of your home page. Stories can be listed by topic or by the students' names. Check your district's Internet policy for listing students' names.

The layout for the story should be designed so each page is on a separate screen; this makes it easier for the user to read the story. Be sure to include the word "continue" or an icon directing the reader to the next page of the story.

Word, PowerPoint, and Hyper Studio can be used to create electronic stories. The degree of interactivity varies depending on the software program. Save all files in an .HTML format. If students are going to create read-along stories or use background music, connect the user to Internet sites where they can download multimedia software.

Students can draw their own pictures to illustrate their stories (see Figure 7.1) using PhotoShop or Paint. Keep the file sizes small so that the stories will not take too long to load.

Example of an Electronic Story

Sequoia Elementary Library in Pleasant Hill, California
<http://www.mdusd.k12.ca.us/sequoiaelementary/library.html>

Figure 7.1 Student Illustrations

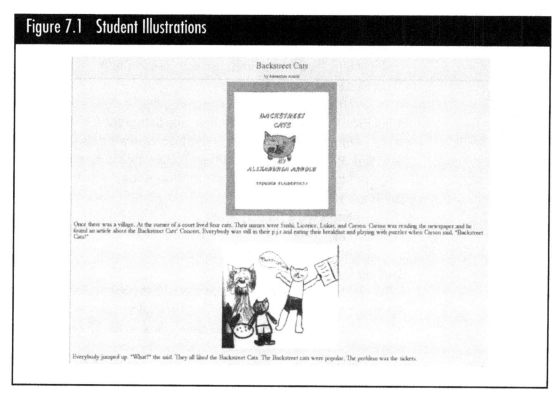

Sequoia Elementary Library in Pleasant Hill, California

Promoting Electronic Stories

This is another example where word of mouth is your best advertisement. Students are going to tell their parents and friends to check out their stories on the library's home page. This will focus attention on your services and programs that promote reading and student learning.

Reader's Advisory Pages

Reading for pleasure encourages literacy and reading as a lifelong habit. Encourage this activity by providing reader's advisory lists, virtual book tours, and book reviews written by your students and teachers, accessed through your home page. These electronic reader's advisory services will assist your students and teachers when they need suggestions for a good book.

Reader's Advisory List

Provide lists of all genres from classics, to horror stories and mysteries, to multicultural literature. These can be developed from:

- Lists published in local newspapers and professional journals.
- Newbery and Caldecott Medal books
- Recommended reading lists for each grade level.
- Best book nominated by the students and faculty.
- Theme-of-the-month book lists such as Women's History Month, Black History Month and national and seasonal holidays.

The following lists will help in planning your reader's advisory page:
Seussville
    <http://www.randomhouse.com/seussville/>
Children's Book Council
    <http://www.cbcbooks.org/>
Orbis Pictus Award for Outstanding Nonfiction for Children
    <http://www.ncte.org/elem/orbispictus/winners.shtml>
New York Public Libraries 100 Best Picture Books Everyone Should Know
    <http://www.nypl.org/branch/kids/gloria.html>
The Book Hive
    <http://www.bookhive.org/>
The Reading Corner
    <http://ccpl.carr.lib.md.us/read/>
Reading Rainbow Booklists
    <http://gpn.unl.edu/rainbow/booklist/booklist.asp>
Scholastic's Magic School Bus, Captain Underpants and others at
    <http://www.scholastic.com/magicschoolbus/home.htm>
Just For Kids Who Love Books
    <http://www3.sympatico.ca/alanbrown/kids.htm>
Grow A Reader Booklist
    <http://www.kidbibs.com/growareader/index.html>
ERIC's Children's Literature Online
    <http://eric.indiana.edu/www/indexwr.html>

As an alternative to posting lists of books, give students a taste of a chapter of a book and hook them into reading. For example, you can subscribe to Chapter A Day Book Club at <http://www.chapteraday.com/>. This company e-mails a five-minute segment each day of a book to subscribers so that by the end of the week readers have read two to three chapters. The following week introduces another book to readers, thus hooking them into a story and consequently into reading. Reading a few pages a day does not seem as overwhelming as reading a whole book. The company also provides a link to the student's school library and to the local public libraries that have their collection online so that students can reserve the books in which they are interested.

Design Considerations for the Reader's Advisory Page
Organize your reading lists in a format that will make for easy access such as grade level, theme, or awards (see Figure 7.2).

Spice up the page by decorating it with book covers of some of the books on your list. Don't worry about violating copyright laws because you are using photos of the book covers for an educational purpose (Russell, Jan. 2002). Remember to keep the picture files small so they do not take too long to load. List the reader's advisory page on your reading page. Provide a link to the book review section of your page so that readers can get an idea of what the book is about. Don't forget to include navigational buttons to return the user to the index of your home page.

Figure 7.2   Format for Organizing Reading Lists

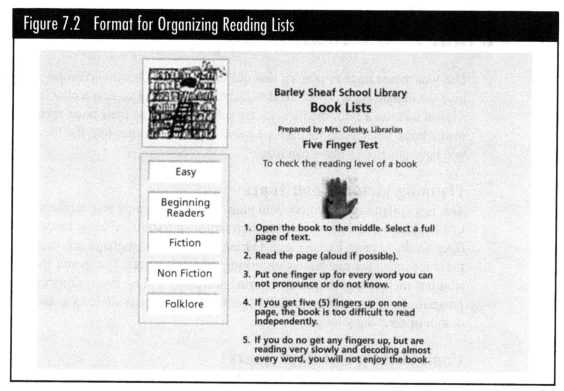

Barley Sheaf Elementary School in Flemington, New Jersey

Examples of Reader's Advisory Pages

Barley Sheaf Elementary School in Flemington, New Jersey
<http://www.frsd.k12.nj.us/barleylibrary/>
Pershing Middle School Library in Houston, Texas
<http://www.pershinglibrary.org/>
Father John V. Doyle School in Coventry, Rhode Island
<http://www.ri.net/RInet/Fr_Doyle/library.html>
Stetson Middle School Library in Philadelphia, Pennsylvania
<http://www.sldirectory.com/stetson.html>
Lancaster High School Media Center in Lancaster, South Carolina
<http://www.lcsd.k12.sc.us/lt/lhs/hp.nsf/HomePages/media>
Timpanogas High School in Timpanogas, Utah
<http://www.alpine.k12.ut.us/THS/media/>
E.O. Lovett Elementary School in Houston, Texas
<http://es.houstonisd.org/LovettES/Library/lovett_library.htm>

Promoting the Reader's Advisory Page

Let your students and teachers know about this service through your school's daily announcements. Refer students and teachers to your reader's advisory list whenever they ask for help in finding a book to read.

Virtual Book Tours

Use your home page to jazz up that old book report! Create virtual book tours that combine the classic book report, reader's advisory, and multimedia technology. Students read a novel and use a multimedia software program to write their book reports. These multimedia book reports can be used whenever a student comes into the library and asks, "Do you have any books that I can read?"

Planning Virtual Book Tours

This is a collaborative project with your school's language arts teachers. Creating a virtual book tour involves more time than writing a traditional book report, so allow at least three weeks to complete the unit. During the unit, the language arts teacher works with the students on the mechanics of writing the book report. The media specialist's responsibilities include instruction on Internet searching and on the multimedia presentation program. Both the media specialist and the teacher assist students in the layout and design of their book tour.

Content of Virtual Book Tours

Students use pictures and text to illustrate and describe the plot, characters, themes, and conflicts in the novels. The last page of each virtual book tour includes the author's biography, author Web sites, the number of pages, and the call number of the book. Students can include an online feedback form asking other students to submit their opinions on the novel.

Design Considerations for Virtual Book Tours

Place the link for the virtual book tours on the reading section of your home page as part of your reader's advisory service.

The virtual book tour can be created using Word or a multimedia software program such as PowerPoint or a Web-authoring program such as FrontPage. Regardless of the program, all files are saved in an .HTML format.

The layout for each book tour starts with the picture of the book jacket. Students can design their own book jackets or use the novel's book jacket. If using the novel's book jacket, there is no violation of copyright laws because the students are using them for educational and not financial purposes. Furthermore, as Carrie Russell states in her article on copyright, "the library is merely trying to promote reading … (and) the copyright holder's ability to market the work has not been harmed—and, indeed, may have been helped." (2002) Book jackets can be downloaded from the Internet or scanned using PhotoShop or Paint. As always, images are saved in a .jpeg or .gif format.

The book's plot, characters, themes, and other information can be placed to the left or right of the book jacket. In designing the virtual book tour, each page should occupy one screen. Be sure to provide navigational tools to direct the reader to each section of the virtual book tour and to the index of your home page.

Promoting Virtual Book Tours

There are several ways to promote your virtual book tours. First, e-mail teachers and let them know about this new reader's advisory service; be sure to include a list of the books on the virtual book tours. Second, whenever students come into the library and ask, "I have to read a book, what can you recommend?" refer them to the virtual book tours. Finally, the students that designed the virtual book tours are going to advertise their accomplishment to other students and their parents, so word of mouth will promote this service, as well as your library.

Online Book Request Form

"Do you have any good books?" This is a perennial question asked by students and faculty. In assisting teachers and students in the book selection process, the goal is to match the person with the right book. This is accomplished by conducting a literary reference interview. A home page can make this literary reference interview more convenient by providing an online form where students and teachers can ask for assistance in finding a good book to read.

Planning an Online Book Request Form
The first step in planning an online book request form is to organize your book lists in the same way as your reader's advisory—by genre, grade level, interest, or reading level. Make sure that your book lists include summaries, which will assist you in making recommendations. Also, bookmark reader's advisories so you have quick access to book reviews.

Next, allot time each day to review requests and to locate books that students might enjoy reading. Allow yourself at least 10 minutes per form. This is probably the same amount of time that you use during a face-to-face request. Be sure to include a disclaimer on your online form that states that this service is for the students and staff of your school; there are not enough hours in the day to provide this service to everyone who submits a request.

Finally, when you e-mail suggested books to students and teachers include the book's call number as this will make it convenient for them. If your catalog is online, remind the student or teacher that they can reserve the book online and get it the next day. If the book they need is not in your collection, remind them that you can borrow it from another library.

Content of the Online Book Request Form
Find out as much information as possible about the student or teacher's reading preferences.
The following items are suggested content for your form (see Figure 7. 3):

Name, Grade
E-mail Address
Interests
Hobbies
Genre
Favorite Authors
A book you enjoyed and the reason why you enjoyed it.
Date Needed By
Page Limit

Figure 7.3 Online Book Request Form

Washington Township High School IMC
Online Book Request Form

This service is provided to the students and staff of Washington Township High School. In order to help you find a book that you will enjoy reading, please complete and submit the following form. You can expect an answer to your request within 24 hours during school days.

Ms. Hill AHill@wtps.org   Mrs. Fisher JFisher@wtps.org

Name	
e-mail address	
Grade or Subject	
Last date the book will be needed	
List two of your favorite authors	
List one book that you enjoyed and tell us why you enjoyed reading it	
Check the boxes for the types of books that you enjoy reading	○ Adventures ○ Fantasy ○ Science Fiction ○ Horror ○ Mysteries ○ Sports ○ Romance ○ Humor ○ Historical Fiction ○ Family Stories
Check the box for the total number of pages	○ 150 ○ 200 ○ doesn't matter

[Submit] [Reset]
Return to Reading Index

Return to IMC Home Page

Return to High School   District

Washington Township High School in Sewell, New Jersey

Design Considerations for the Online Book Request Form

Place the link for the online book request form on the reader's advisory section of your home page. Placing the link here will allow students and teachers to view the other reader's advisory services that you offer on your home page.

Don't worry about creating forms because most Web-authoring programs include form makers, or you can use a form maker found on the Internet. Always include your name and e-mail address on the form so users know whom to contact. As with other sections of your home page, include navigational tools so users can get back to the reader's advisory page and index of your home page.

Example of an Online Book Request Form

Washington Township High School IMC in Sewell, New Jersey
<http://www.wtps.org/wths/imc/index.html>

Promoting the Online Book Request Form

Advertise this service in your principal's newsletter, as well as in your library's newsletters and bulletin board displays. E-mail teachers asking them to alert their students about the online book request form whenever they assign books to read.

Student Book Reviews

Book reviews are another reader's advisory service that can be offered on the reading section of your home page. It is a wonderful way for students to share the books they enjoyed with other students and help them decide if they want to read the same book. It is also an opportunity for students to learn about books they may not otherwise have read. An added plus to student book reviews is that they foster good writing skills as well as promoting reading.

Planning the Student Book Review Page

Collaborate with the language arts teachers and have their students submit book reviews for the home page. If you have a book club, encourage members to submit book reviews.

Use interactive forms for the submission of the reviews. Design separate forms based on the age level of the writer (see Figures 7.4 and 7.5). Make sure you add a disclaimer to your book review page that these reviews are solely the opinions of the writer and do not reflect the opinions of the school district.

Design Considerations for the Student Book Review Page

Organize these reviews by student name, grade level, genre or title of the book (see Figure 7.6). If you do use student names, check your district's policy as most districts only permit the use of students' first name and initial of the last name. Archive your student book reviews alphabetically by title of the work. The link for this archive is placed directly below the book reviews.

Use public domain pictures of books and of children reading books to decorate the book review page. Scan the dust jacket of each book that is being reviewed so there is visual connection with the text. Again, keep the pictures small so that the page will download quickly. Remember to put navigational tools from the reading page to the reader's advisory and the book review page. Place the link for student book reviews on the reading section under reader's advisory. Finally, as a service to your teachers, administrators, and students, provide links to other book review sites, such as the following, on the Internet.

Book Page
<http://www.bookpage.com>
Boston Globe Online Book Review
<http://www.boston.com/globe/living/bookreviews/>
The New York Times Book Review
<http://www.nytimes.com/pages/books/>

Examples of Student Book Review Pages

The Woodlands High School's McCullough Campus in Woodlands, Texas
<http://info.conroe.isd.tenet.edu/senior/mccullough/TWHS-McClibrary/>
Athena Media Center in Rochester, New York
<http://www.greece.k12.ny.us/ath/library/>
National Cathedral Upper School in Mt. St. Alban's, Washington, D.C.
<http://ncs.cathedral.org/uslibrary/Library/cybercafe/booklovers.htm>

Figure 7.4   Online Interactive Book Review Form for Younger Students

Write a Book Review

Write a book review that will be used by other students in the school whenever they need to find a book to read. Proofread your book review for spelling and grammar before you submit it.

Your First Name and Initial of Last Name

Grade

Title of Book

Author of Book

What is your opinion of the book?
◎ Super   ◎ Good   ◎ OK   ◎ Awful

What was your favorite character and why did you like this one?

Write a summary of the story; don't give away the ending.

Would you recommend this book to a friend?
◎ Yes   ◎ No

SUBMIT   CLEAR

St. Nudgee College Library in QLD, Australia
<http://www.nudgee.com/library/recommen.htm>
Alpha Intermediate School Library in Morristown, Tennessee
<http://www.hcboe.net/Main/School/AI/lib/libindex.html>
Dallas High School in Dallas, Oregon
<http://www.open.org/~dallashs/GoodReads.html>
Franklin County High School Library Media Center in Frankfort, Kentucky
<http://www.franklin.k12.ky.us/fchs/fchslibrary/index.htm>
Vineland Library Media Center in Retonda West, Florida
<http://www.ccps.k12.fl.us/Schools/VES/reviews.htm>
Father John V. Doyle School Library in Coventry, Rhode Island
<http://www.ri.net/RInet/Fr_Doyle/library.html>
Stetson Middle School Library in Philadelphia, Pennsylvania
<http://www.sldirectory.com/stetson.html>
Sinott Magnet School in Brooklyn, New York
<http://www.angelfire.com/ny2/library218/>
Ganada High School Library in Walworth, New York
<http://www.gananda.org/library/mshslibrary/indexgcl.htm>
Palmerston Resource Center in Palmerston, Australia
<http://www.palmdps.act.edu.au/library/resource_centremain.htm>

Promoting the Student Book Review Page

As with other sections of your reader's advisory page, whenever a student or teacher needs a recommendation for a book, refer them to the online book review page. Students who have written these reviews will also talk about them to their parents and friends, thereby promoting your home page and the services of your library.

Special Reading Events

Promote reading by staging reading activities in your library. These can range from competitions to marathon read-ins to author visits. Organizing reading promotions requires a lot of planning, but students will love participating and it will generate positive publicity for your library program and promote lifelong reading.

Read-In

In recent years, Seattle, Chicago, Philadelphia, and other cities have realized the impact of reading in people lives and have actively promoted the importance of reading by organizing read-ins. A read-in occurs when a community selects a book and everyone in the community is encouraged to read that book over a certain time period. Ideally, the read-in encourages the school community to discuss the book in class, in the cafeteria, in the library, and at the dinner table. What a wonderful way for your library and its home page to help foster a sense of community and at the same time encourage reading.

Figure 7.5   Write a Book Review

Write a Book Review

Parents, Teachers, and Students: Please share a great book you have read with us by completing this form.

Your First Name and Initial of Last Name

Your E-mail Address

Student   Grade   ⬭

Teacher   ⬭

Parent   ⬭

Title of Book

Author of Book

Genre of Book

Was this book made into a movie?   ◉ Yes   ◉ No

Would this book make a good movie?   ◉ Yes   ◉ No

Review (no more than 10 sentences please!)

Overall rating

One Star   ⬭   ☆

Two Stars   ⬭   ☆   ☆

Three Stars   ⬭   ☆   ☆   ☆

Four Stars   ⬭   ☆   ☆   ☆   ☆

Five Stars   ⬭   ☆   ☆   ☆   ☆   ☆

SUBMIT   CLEAR

Figure 7.6 Organizational Format of a Student Book Review Page

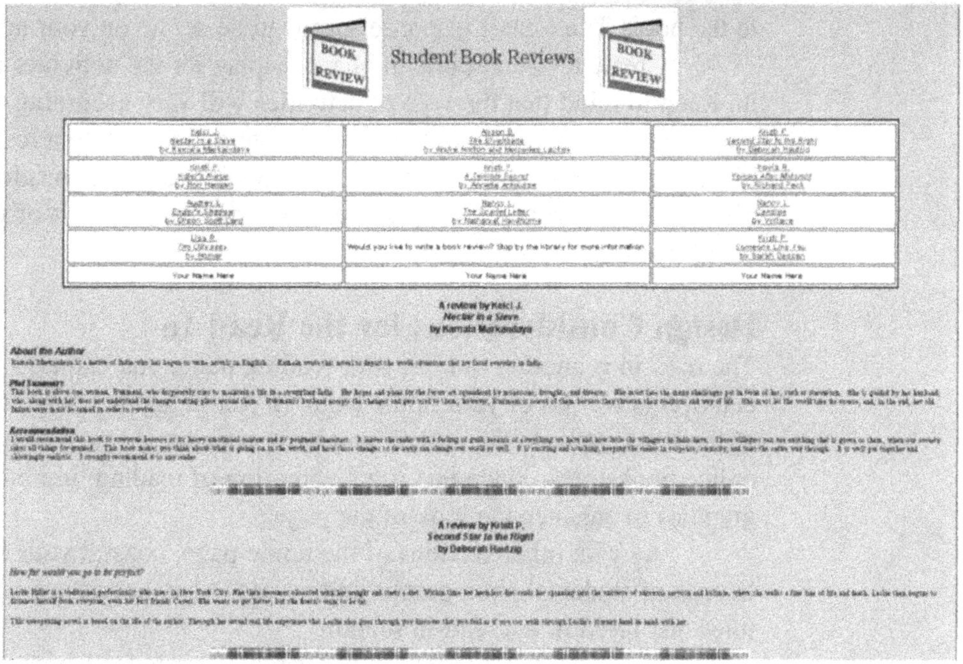

The Woodlands High School in Woodlands, Texas

Planning the Read-In

The first step in sponsoring a read-in is to form a committee of parents, students, teachers, and administrators to select 25 books that the community would enjoy reading. Direct the committee members to your home page so they can access the book list and book reviews to assist them in selecting books for the read-in. Remember that you will also have an additional role as a literary consultant who answers any questions that arise about the various books. Once the committee has selected 25 titles for your school, design a read-in voting ballot so students, teachers, and parents can vote for the top three books they would like to read. The ballot is distributed in the principal's newsletter and on your home page. The committee tabulates the ballots and the entire school community reads the book that receives the most votes.

Next, notify the public libraries and local bookstores about the selected title so they can stock up on the book. Finally, set time limits for the read-in. The grade level of your school will determine the time limits. For example, in an elementary school the chosen book may take a week to read, whereas in a high school the chosen book would require a longer time period. During the read-in collaborate with the language arts teachers and have them spend a few minutes each day discussing the book with their students.

Content of the Read-In

Here are some ideas for your read-in:

Work with your language arts, reading, and graphic arts teachers and have their students design posters and bookmarks that will be displayed throughout the school and on your home page.

Encourage parents to take a night off and read with their children. After they have completed the book, have them e-mail the library with their thoughts and reactions to the book. The e-mail response form can be set up on your home page.

Create a virtual bulletin board display for the activities associated with the read-in. Keep in mind that the type of activities will vary according to grade level. For example, in an elementary school, you can invite the parents to a reading party in your library. In a middle or high school, your book club can sponsor a read-in party as an after-school activity. All of these activities can become part of your virtual bulletin board display.

Design Considerations for the Read-In

The read-in is another link on your reading page; you can also create a link to the special events section of your home page. In designing this page, be sure to include a photo of the book, links to the author, and book reviews. As a convenience include links to online bookstores. Since this is a celebration of reading, use bright, festive colors and graphics to enhance the look of the page.

As with other sections of the home page, consult your district's policy regarding the use of students' photographs and names. Also, keep the file sizes small for all pictures displayed in the read-in section.

If you are including read-in response forms for parent, teacher, and student comments on the book, be sure to display your e-mail address and directions prominently on the page, and remember to include navigational tools directing the users to the different sections of your home page.

Promoting the Read-In

This event is given full media treatment with ads about the book and the read-in dates appearing in local papers, on local television stations as well as in the principal's newsletter and the library's informational literature and home page. Use the morning announcements to publicize the read-in and direct the school community to your library's home page to learn about the read-in activities. During the read-in, word of mouth will promote the event as the book is read and discussed by teachers, students, administrators, and parents.

Reading Competitions

Introduction

Reading competitions are another way to encourage students to read and at the same time showcase the many activities your library sponsors that promote reading and literacy. The purpose of reading competitions is to promote a love of reading and to create a sense of excitement in the school. Students can compete in reading competitions organized on the state and national level such as the Battle of the Books or Reading Olympics, or you can design your own competitions to make your home page the center for these competitions.

Planning Reading Competitions

Organize your competitions using the same framework provided by national and state competitions. This means forming teams of 10–12 students who compete with other

Monticello Library Media Center in Longview, Washington

teams either within the school or with other schools locally or nationally. One format includes online quizzes based on the plot and summary. This type of competition encourages students to read a variety of books and retain information about the plot, characters, and setting of the books. Participants have to respond to questions about incidents in the book by identifying its author and title. Another type of reading competition involves reading the most books, pages, minutes or hours in a given time period.

Make sure you order enough books for the participants and alert the public libraries and bookstores of the events so they can reserve the books for your students.

Content of Reading Competitions

Since your library's home page is the center for the competition, post the rules, the number of books, the titles that have to be read, and the competition dates. Pique interest in the competition by posting a Riddle of the Day or a Reading Question, which relates to the reading competitions on your home page.

At the end of the competition post the names of the students and the teams who won first, second, or third place along with their photographs. Follow your district's policy regarding the publication of student photos. As with other special events, videotape or create a bulletin board display of the activities during the competition.

Design Considerations for Reading Competitions

Use a catchy name if you are designing your own competition or use the national or state competition names such as Read a Ton, Battle of the Books, or Reading Olympics. Locate the competition on a prominent place on your home page (see Figures 7.7 and 7.8). Use a table or list to display the various activities of your reading competition. Scan dust jackets and use student-designed reading graphics to make the page visually appealing.

Increase visitors to your home page by placing the reading competitions link on your reading page, your special events page, and the index of your home page.

If you are using videotape displays of your reading competitions, post links to Internet sites, such as the following, where free viewers can be downloaded.

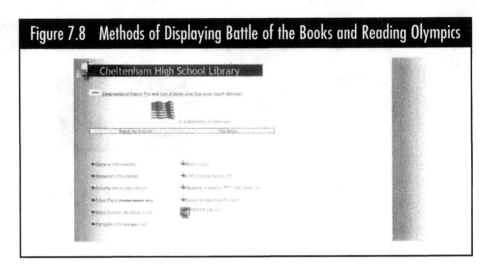

Cheltenham High School in Wyncotte, Pennsylvania

QuickTime Pro
> <http://www.apple.com/quicktime/>

Multimedia Xplorer
> <http://www.moonsoftware.com/>

MPEG Player
> <http://www.mpeg.org/MPEG/MSSG/>

Examples of Reading Competitions

Monticello Library Media Center in Longview, Washington
> <http://www.longview.k12.wa.us/mont/LMCHpg/bob.htm>

Cheltenham High School Library in Wyncotte, Pennsylvania
> <http://mciunix.mciu.k12.pa.us/~chsweb/>

Edna M. Fielder Elementary School in Katy, Texas
> <http://www.katy.isd.tenet.edu/fe/library/fielderlibrary/readingincentive
> programs.html>

Georgia O'Keefe Elementary School in Albuquerque, New Mexico
> <http://www.okeeffe.aps.edu/Okeeffe_Web/library/default.html>

Promoting Reading Competitions

Include information about the reading competitions in the principal's newsletter so parents are aware of these events. Students can check their team's standing in the reading competition by accessing the library's home page during their language arts classes. Use the morning announcements to encourage students to check your home page for the Reading Competition Question or Riddle of the Day.

Virtual Author Visits

An author visit is another way to connect students to reading and books. It promotes the library as an exciting place for students, provides opportunities to extend the collaborative process, and promotes the library and its programs and services. Author visits are such popular events that it is disappointing that not all students can participate. A home page allows all students in your school to participate virtually in this special event.

Content of Virtual Author Visits

The following are suggestions for author visits:

- Videotape and post the author visit on your home page. Check with the author to see whether this is permitted without paying an additional fee. Be sure to obtain the author's release form.
- Post an online question form so students can submit questions to the author. Make sure that the author gets these questions before the visit so the author's responses can be posted as soon as possible after the visit.
- Be sure to obtain permission to post the author's photo and biography, dust jackets of books, and links to the author's home page.
- Create a virtual bulletin board display of pictures taken during the author's visit and book-related projects developed from the visit.
- Design contests based on the author's books, which can range from designing bookmarks and book covers to treasure hunts and trivia.
- Post student reviews of the author's books.

Planning the Virtual Author Visit

Creating a virtual author visit page begins well in advance of the actual visit. Collaborate with your language arts, graphic design, and art teachers to design student activities that coordinate with the books written by the visiting author. Allow at least two weeks to organize and post the contests, book reviews, author information, and online question forms to your home page.

Design Considerations for the Virtual Author Visit

Create a link on the reading page of your home page for your author visit. If you have a special events page list the author visit there as well. The author information is the first link on this page. You can save time by downloading pictures from the author's home page instead of scanning them into Paint or PhotoShop.

If you are going to use interactive forms for contests or online questions, download these from the Internet. Templates for forms are also included in your Web-authoring program.

As with the other sections of your home page, keep picture files small and include navigational tools so users can get from the virtual author visit page to the index of your reading page and home page.

Examples of Virtual Author Visits

Norfeldt Media Center West Hartford, Connecticut
<http://www.whps.org/schools/norfeldt/libraryweb/>
Van Buren Elementary School Instructional Media Center in Cedar Rapids, Iowa
<http://www.cr.k12.ia.us/vanb/loreenleedy.html>
Woodruff Library Media Center in Berkeley Heights, New Jersey
<http://www.columbia.bhs.k12.nj.us/woodlibrary/edmyersvisit.html>
Hamilton South Elementary School Media Center in Lockbourne, Ohio
<http://www.hamilton-local.k12.oh.us/pub/hlsd/SO/sohome/media_center.htm#author>

Promoting the Virtual Author Visit

Author visits are media events that are highly publicized in local newspapers and on television. Your library's URL should be included on any promotional articles you send to newspapers. Since you are working with your school's language arts teachers, e-mail them daily to notify them of additions to the author section of your home page. If you are posting contests to your home page as an author visit activity, use your school's daily announcements to alert students that they can win a prize by going to the library's home page and competing in an online contest.

Online Book Club

There is an upsurge in reading. Readers are turning to books to find reflective solitude and peace from the stress of their fast-paced lives. Perhaps Oprah's book club was the catalyst for this change. Maybe the aroma of Starbucks and chatter from book discussion groups lure readers into stores such as Barnes & Noble and Borders, or maybe it's the popularity of book clubs in public libraries. Media specialists need to use similar promotional activities to entice students into browsing the aisles of the library for great books. We need to promote our school libraries as community centers where students and staff can join book clubs and discuss books and interact with one another. Many students and faculty enjoy interacting outside the classroom and the library provides the perfect place where they can discuss literature, and gain new insights and fresh perspectives from each other.

While many students and teachers may be able to participate in an after-school book club in your library, this may not be possible for others because of scheduling conflicts. This problem can be resolved by hosting an online book club on your home page. Online book clubs are especially convenient in our fast-paced society when students and teachers want to discuss books with others, but cannot always find the time to do so.

Planning the Online Book Club

To get an online book club off the ground, select a few books from all genres and levels that would appeal to both teachers and students. Then ask students and teachers to select the books they want to read and discuss during the online book club. Make sure you post the book list and the book discussion dates on your home page so readers can plan ahead and make time to read them. Organize the online book club by grade, genres, classics, multicultural titles, interests, or hobbies.

Don't forget to give your local bookstores and libraries the titles of the books that have been selected for the online book club so they can have enough copies on hand.

The easiest way to start your book club is to limit participants to teachers, students, and staff in your own school. With more experience you can expand the book club to other schools in your state, nationally, or even internationally.

Set up your online book club as a listserv or a chat room. There are advantages and disadvantages to each option. The advantage of an online chat room is that the participants can share their opinions in real time and the discussions are often lively and unpredictable. The disadvantage is there is a set time for the online book discussion and this may not be convenient for all participants. In comparison, a listserv has no scheduled time period for the discussion, thus allowing the participants to discuss the book at a time that is convenient for them and to access any discussions they have missed. The disadvantage of a listserv is the loss of spontaneity that occurs in a chat room.

Set a time frame for each online book discussion. Limit each discussion to a one-month period. If you start the club in September and end it in June, there will be 10 book discussions per year. If using a chat room format, determine an online meeting time that is convenient for all members.

If you are conducting the online book club using a chat room format, you will have to select a moderator to lead the discussion. Usually this is a librarian, but here is an opportunity to extend the collaborative process by sharing the responsibilities with the other teachers in your school. Invite teachers to volunteer to lead the discussion for the book of their choice. Be sure to provide them with guidelines for online book discussions.

Design Considerations for the Online Book Club

The online book club is a separate category on your reading page. List the titles of the books along with pictures of their dust jackets and the dates for discussion of each book. If you are using a chat room format, make sure to post the exact time of the online chat. Don't worry about creating your own chat room. You can use AOL's Instant Messenger or Talk City. Just locate a link to this site on your online book club page.

Parachat
    <http://parachat.com>
America Online
    <http://groups.aol.com/>

If you are using a listserv format, you will need to acquire a commercial software product that you will use to create a group e-mail list of participants, similar to LM-NET. Secure administrative approval for the listserv. Be sure to include directions on how to subscribe to the listserv. Limit the discussion to a specific time frame. This can range anywhere from two weeks to a month. Make sure you add a disclaimer to your page reminding users of the proper netiquette when they are in the chat room or on a listserv. The following are listserv software programs:

L-Soft International, which is a fee-based service.
    <http://www.lsoft.com>
Majordomo, from Great Circle Associates, which is freeware.
    <http://www.greatcircle.com>

Post the link for the online book club on your reading page and on the index of your home page. Archive past book discussions on your home page chronologically by title and by date.

Decorate this page with book covers from the Internet or scan covers into Paint or PhotoShop. You can also design a logo for the online book club to use on this page, which can be as simple as a public domain graphic or a student creation.

Examples of Online Book Clubs

Athena Media Center in Rochester, New York
                            <http://www.greece.k12.ny.us/ath/library/>
Hastings Ninth Grade Center in Houston, Texas
                            <http://www.alief.isd.tenet.edu/hastings-ngc/Default.htm>
Central Learning Resource Center in Duncanville, Texas
                            <http://www.duncanville.k12.tx.us/dcavitt/>
Aikin Elementary School Library in Paris, Texas
                            <http://www.parisisd.net/aikin/library.htm>
Sehome High School Library in Bellington, Washington
                            <http://wwwshs1.bham.wednet.edu/curric/cool/books.htm>

Promoting the Online Book Club

Newsletters and announcements on the public address system are some of the ways the online book club can be promoted. Advertise the online book club through articles in the school's newsletter, which is distributed in the community as well as throughout the school. Target school activities such as the Foreign Language club, which might want to form a multicultural online book club. E-mail reminders are another effective way of promotion. Create a group e-mail and send weekly reminders of the book to be read and the times of the discussions to students, teachers, and administrators. Use the dust jacket of the book of the month as screen savers on your library's computers to promote the online book clubs. Send flyers home with students and make announcements over the public announcement systems. You can also place a banner on your home page to announce the current book being read.

Summer Reading

When the school bell rings for the final time for the summer holidays, it signals a time for students to participate in many leisure activities, including reading. Now they have the time to read the books that interest them rather than the ones required for school. Since school libraries are closed during the summer and the librarian is not there to plug a great book, a home page with its reader's advisories and links to summer reading programs takes over as a virtual librarian.

Content of the Summer Reading Page

Post the required summer reading lists for your school and book reviews to help students decide which books they want to read. As an added service, post links to bookstores and libraries where students can obtain these books, and remember to follow school and library board policies when posting links to commercial sites.

Provide a variety of reading lists on different subjects for your students. These lists allow students to select books they are interested in rather than what they are required to read and can serve as the starting point for the students' summer reading. Include links to your reader's advisory pages.

Establish a summer book exchange on your home page. Students and teachers bring the books they want to exchange to the library. Advertise the titles of these books on your home page.

Sponsor a summer reading program that awards prizes to students based on the number of books they read. Parents complete a form verifying the number of books read by their children and the students return this form in September and receive prizes such as certificates to fast food restaurants, amusement parks, ball games, movies, and bookstores. Don't forget to list the names of businesses that have contributed prizes on your home page and also the names of the students and the number of books they have read. Remember to follow your district's policy regarding publishing students' names.

Sponsor an "unplugged" summer program. Encourage students to take a pledge not to watch TV for a week or two during the summer. Ask them to keep a journal of their activities during their unplugged week. In September post these activities on your home page.

Create a travelogue of travel books and Web links to different countries. Encourage students to e-mail to your library accounts and photos of their summer travels. Post these on the travelogue page so they can be shared with their classmates.

Provide links to the public library's summer reading and list the names of the students who volunteered at the public library during the summer. This is an expedient opportunity to combine forces and collaborate with the public library and coordinate your program with theirs. Don't forget to follow your district's policy regarding publishing students' names.

Design Considerations for the Summer Reading Page

This page lends itself to a more creative approach. Decorate it with colorful summer graphics. Use a consistent format for the colors, graphics, and font styles for each section of your summer reading page.

Organize your summer reading lists by grade level, genre, interests, or hobbies (see Figure 7.9). Format the content as an alphabetically arranged table. Add photos of students' summer reading activities and as always make sure that the files are saved in a

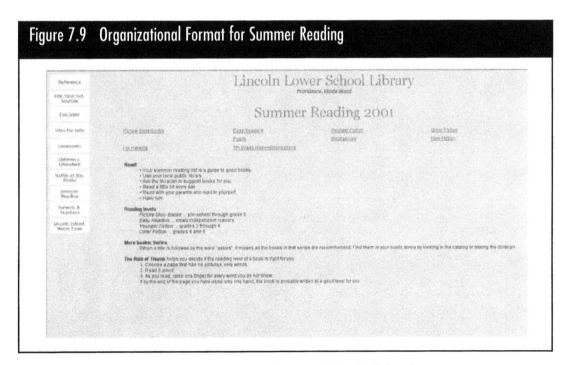

Figure 7.9   Organizational Format for Summer Reading

Lincoln Lower School Library in Providence, Rhode Island

.jpeg or .gif format; be sure to keep the file small so the page loads quickly. Don't forget to follow your district's policy regarding publishing students' names and photos on the Web. Remember to include navigational tools directing users to your reading page and to the index of your home page.

Examples of Summer Reading Pages

Lincoln Lower School Library in Providence, Rhode Island
<http://www.lincolnschool.org/Libraries/SummerReading/SRInfo.html>
The Edna M. Fielder Elementary School Library Media Center in Katy, Texas
<http://www.katy.isd.tenet.edu/fe/library/fielderlibrary/Summer_
Reading_List.html>
The Paideia High School Library in Atlanta, Georgia
<http://www.paideiaschool.org/library/reading.htm>
Concord Elementary School in Anderson, South Carolina
<http://concord.anderson5.net/library/>
Crofton Middle School in Crofton, Maryland
<http://www.aacps.org/aacps/croftms/cmslibrary.htm>
Lisbon Elementary School in Lisbon, Maryland
<http://www.howard.k12.md.us/lisbon/default.html>

Promoting the Summer Reading Page

Send flyers home with students alerting parents to check the home page for all reading activities over the summer. Remind students via morning announcements to come to the library before the end of the school year to check out books for the summer.

Chapter Eight

Conclusion

Though the ideas presented in this book are easily adaptable to any library, we realize that an individual library cannot possibly have a home page with every single resource that we have discussed. Since each library's home page should be a reflection of the community it serves, it should include resources or links to resources that will benefit the community and the school's curriculum. Therefore, you should begin with relevant curriculum needs, community resources, and special events in your library. A good way to assess what your community requires is to use the needs assessment surveys that are included in this book. If you conduct the assessment at the beginning of the school year, you will have time to decide what to incorporate in your home page and how to design it during the year.

The time needed to design and create a home page will vary according to how much or how little you intend to include in your home page. Initially, it took us three days to design our home page (i.e., deciding on the content, the colors, researching good Web sites, and uploading the information to our server). After those tasks were completed we added more links and checked for broken links periodically. Now we try to check for broken links at least once a month since it is necessary to update these to remain credible. Your home page should also include a disclaimer stating that though you are providing links to certain sites as a service, your library does not endorse any views, facts, or commercial products that may be offered on these sites.

Throughout this book we introduced ways to harness the power of the Internet to promote your library program. Although policy issues were only mentioned in passing, it is important to be aware of guidelines that are indigenous to each library setting. Does the school or library board have a Web publishing policy? Does it have a virtual collection development policy? Does it have an acceptable use policy? It is necessary to be cognizant of these policies as you begin the process of designing your home page and to keep abreast of any policy changes. Since a home page is a constantly evolving information source, keeping up to date with policy issues affecting your home page should also be an ongoing process.

Just as businesses have taken advantage of technological advances to create their own home pages to market their companies, librarians need to market themselves by using the same multimedia tools that have been successful in the business world. A home page publicizes libraries and their programs to communities, schools, patrons, and most importantly, taxpayers, 24 hours a day. This electronic presence is essential for 21st century librarians to not only to stay current with technological developments, but also to promote themselves to their community. This virtual promotion is essential especially during times of budget cuts and belt tightening.

The task of creating a home page may seem daunting, but it really isn't. Once it has been created, you will be pleased with the favorable response by students and faculty. You will probably wonder how you ever managed without one. Your home page will become a valuable tool to enhance, not replace, the print resources used in the library. At the same time, it will provide global visibility for all the programs and services that your library provides. If a picture is worth a thousand words, a home page with its multimedia elements will have an even greater impact. By building and promoting a home page you will be in the public's eye all of the time. Your home page will trumpet your library program all year round, instead of just during National Library Week. So, happy cyber designing and good luck as you toot your own horn!

Appendix
List of Figures and Permissions

Figure 1.1   Editorial cartoon reprinted with permission of Ed Stein from *The Rocky Mountain News*

Figure 1.2   Teacher Survey

Figure 1.3   Student Survey

Figure 1.4   Parent Survey

Figure 1.5   Public Library Survey

Figure 2.1   Library Reservation Calendar

Figure 2.2   Technology Survey

Figure 2.3   Workshop Template

Figure 2.4   Workshop Evaluation Form

Figure 3.1   Sample Frames Format

Figure 3.2   Web Site Evaluation Form

Figure 3.3   Sample Format for an Online Style Manual

Figure 3.4   Screen shot published with permission of Ann Hill and Julieta Dias Fisher from Washington Township High School

Figure 3.5   Ask a Librarian Form

Figure 4.1   Screen shot published with permission of Cynthia (Sam) Foley from Buckley Elementary School

Figure 4.2   Screen shot published with permission of James Maxwell from Castro Valley High School Cybrary

Figure 4.3   Screen shot published with permission of Linda Herward from Falk School Library

Figure 4.4   Screen shot published with permission of Cassandra Barnett from Fayetteville High School Library

Figure 5.1   Screen shot published with permission of Susan Geiger from Moreau Catholic High School Library

Figure 5.2   Screen shot published with permission of D'Etta Broam from Midway Elementary School Media Center

Bibliography

American Association of School Librarians and Association for Educational Communications and Technology. *Information Power: Building Partnerships for Learning*. Chicago: ALA, 1998.

Adubato, Steve. "Dealing with the Media — and Winning." *Business News New Jersey* 27 Nov. 2001: 34.

Balas, Janet. "If You Build It, Will They Come?" *Computers in Libraries* Sept. 2000: 60–63.

———. "Reading is 'In'." *Computers in Libraries* Sept. 2001: 64–67.

Ballard, Susan, comp. and ed. *Count On Reading: Tips For Planning Reading Motivation Programs Handbook*. American Library Association, 1997.

Barks, Edward J. "To Web or not to Web?" *Public Relations Tactics* Aug. 1999: 6.

Baule, Steven and Laura Bertani. "Marketing 101 for Your Library Media Program." *The Book Report* Nov.–Dec. 2000: 47–49.

Breitkopf, David. "Designs on Websites." *Westchester County Business Journal* 3 July 2000: 11.

Cash, Jr., James I. "IT and PR: Living in Spin." *Information Week* 9 June 1997: 148.

Childers, Thomas. *What's Good?: Discovering your Public Library's Effectiveness*. American Library Association, 1993.

Chiou, Guey-Fa. "Reader Interface of Computer-based Reading Environment." *International Journal of Instructional Media* 122.2 (1995): 121–134.

Clark, Kirsten, "P.R. Strategy Changes as Business Seek Web Presence." *Las Vegas Business Press* 24 Nov. 1997: 12.

Clifford, Lynch. "Electrifying the Book." *Library Journal* 124.17 (1999): 3–7.

Collins, Jim. "How Great Companies Tame Technology." *Newsweek* 29 Apr. 2002: 51.

Colnick, Sandi, ed. *Friends of Libraries Sourcebook*. American Library Association, 1990.

"Computers and Kids." *Reading Today* Aug.–Sept. 2001: 4.

Dianis, Laura K. "Online Journal." *Curriculum Administrator* Aug. 2000: 79.

Dobrez, Cindy and Lynn Rutan. "Mapping March Madness: Here's a Sneaky Way to Lure Kids (Especially Boys) Into The Library." *School Library Journal* Feb. 2002: 43.

Edsall, Marian S. *Practical PR for School Library Media Centers*. Neal-Schuman, 1984.

Evans, David. "Control Freaks." *MC: Marketing Computers* Dec. 1994: 10.

Farmer, Lesley S. J. "Collecting and Using Original Student Work." *The Book Report* Mar.–Apr. 2001: 10–14.

———. "Teaming Parents with Technology" *The Book Report* Jan.–Feb. 2002: 52–53.

Fialkoff, Francine. "Raising Readers." *Library Journal* 1 Aug. 2001: 74.

Fisher, Julieta Dias and Ann Hill. "Showcase Your Library via a Home Page." *The Book Report* Nov.–Dec. 2000: 44–45.

———. "The ABCs of Web Page Design." *Library Talk* Nov.–Dec. 2001: 28–29.

———. "Tooting Your Own Horn: Web Based Public Relations for the School Media Specialist." *Library Talk* May–Jun. 2002: 8–9.

Flagg, Gordon. "Putting the Ad in Advocacy." *American Libraries* 31.6 (2000): 56.

Flannery, Joyce L. "Public Relations Critical Component of Successful Businesses." *San Diego Business Journal* 9 Oct. 2001: 14–16.

Fleck, Jim. *The Wizard's Media Handbook: Profitably Promoting Your Library With the Media*. Fleck Leadership Center, 1995.

Frank, Carolyn R., Dixon, Carol N., Brandts, Lois R. "Bears, Trolls, and Pagemasters: Learning About Learners in Book Clubs." *Reading Teacher* Feb. 2001: 448–463.

Gissen, Willy. "Online Public Relations Pointers." *Westchester County Business Journal* 6 Dec. 1999: 17.

Goetz, Thomas. "Spinning the Web." *Village Voice* 10 Dec. 1996: 27.

Goldstein, Jonathan. "Notes from Chicago the City of Big Shoulders (and Readers)." *The New York Times on the Web* 8 Feb. 2002 <http://www.nytimes.com/2002/02/08/opinion/08GOLD. html?ex=1014183867&ei=1&en=>.

Glock, Norman and Mike Bacon. "Are Assigned Summer Reading Lists Obsolete?" *NEA Today* Feb. 2001: 11.

Hathaway, Jonathan. "Ease your Way into the Infobahn." *Business Journal Serving Southern Tier, CNY, Mohawk Valley, Finger Lakes, North* 14 Oct. 1996: 12SB.

Herring, Mark Y. "Why the Internet Can't Replace the Library." *Education Digest* 67.1 (2001): 46–50.

Hopkins, Deborah, "Taking Care of Business," *Executive Excellence* Jul. 2001: 3–4.

"How Many Online?" *NUA*. Computer Scope Ltd., 2001. 29 Apr. 2002 <http://www.nua.com/surveys/how_many_online/index.html>.

Hudson, Laura. "A New Age of Accessibility." *School Library Journal* Net Connect Supp. Winter 2002: 19–21.

"In the Company of Books." *Independent School* 60.1 (2001): 62–64.

Jordan, Peter. "Becoming a Player in the PR Game." *VARBusiness* 7 Dec. 1998: 129–130.

Krashen, Stephen. *The Power of Reading: Insights from the Research*. Libraries Unlimited, 1993.

Lance, Keith Curry. "Dick and Jane Go to the Head of The Class." *School Library Journal* April 2000: 44–47.

Leverett, Larry. "Extending your Influence by 'Spreading the Word'." *The Book Report* May–June 2001: 24–26.

Lines, Patricia. "Homeschoolers: Estimating Numbers and Growth." United States Department of Education, Spring 1999. 11 Sept. 2001 <http://www.ed.gov/offices/OERI/SAI/homeschool/>.

Logan, Deborah Kay. "Project Page Partnerships: Linking to Collaboration and Learning." *The Book Report* Mar.–Apr. 2001: 48–49.

Majka, David. "The Conqueror Bookworm." *American Libraries* 32.6 (2001): 60–64.

Mcgaugh, Scott. "The Role of PR in Marketing Isn't Spin, It's Glue." San Diego *Business Journal* 10 Sept. 2001: 15.

McGee, Kimberley, "Local PR Agencies Dive into Cyberspace." *Las Vegas Business Press* 3 June 1996: 13.

McElmeel, Sharron L. "Model Web Pages to Inspire You." *Technology Connection* Nov. 1996: 28–30.

McKenzie, Jamie. "Libraries of the Future." *FNO From Now On The Educational Technology Journal* Nov. 1993 < http://www.fno.org/libraries.html>.

Minkel, Walter. "A Chapter a Day." *School Library Journal* 47.5 (2001): 31–33.

——."Get with the Program, Part 2." *School Library Journal* 47.12 (2001): 31.

NUA Internet Surveys. Scope Communications Group, 11 July 2002
   <http://www.nua.com/surveys>.

Newburger, Eric. "Home Computers and Internet Use in the United States: August
   2000." *Current Population Reports, Aug. 2001*. United States Department of
   Census, 3 Feb. 2002. <http://www.census.gov/prod/2001pubs/p23-207.pdf.>

O'Briant, Don. "Read, then Chat: Online Book Clubs Connect Authors, Fans." *Abilene
   Reporter-News* 15 July 2001.
   <http://www.reporternews.com/2001/enter/read0715.htm>.

O'Donovan, Cheryl. "Copyright versus Copywrong." *Communication World* Oct.–Nov.
   2001: 12–16.

Ojala, Marydee. "Online Reading as a Nonlinear Activity." *EContent* Oct.–Nov. 2000: 6.

Orava, Hilkka. "Marketing is an Attitude of Mind." *IFLANET General Conference
   Federation of Library Associations and Institutions* Aug. 31–Sept. 5, 1997: 1–5.

Paul, Pamela. "The Online Reading Room." *American Demographics* June 2001: 34–38.

Pedersen, Knud. "The Network-Book-Club." *Information Services & Use* 17.3 (1997):
   183–187.

Peek, Robin. "A Busy Summer for E-Books." *Information Today* Sept. 2000: 42.

Quinn, Patrick. "Typical Day for a Student in 2030." *The Book Report* Jan.–Feb. 2002:
   16–18.

Reese, Jean. "Education via the Web." *Multimedia Schools* Jan.–Feb. 2000: 47–50.

Rogers, Monica, "Some Low-Cost Tricks to Tout Online Firms." *Crain's Chicago
   Business* 12 Dec. 2000: SB6.

Russell, Carrie. "Is It a Crime to Copy: Libraries Often Use Scans of Book Covers to
   Promote Reading." *School Library Journal* Jan. 2002: 41.

——."Is it Kosher to Copy?: Just Because the Usage is School-Related Doesn't Mean
   It's Legal." *School Library Journal* Feb. 2002: 41.

——. Telephone Interview. 19 Feb. 2002

Samuelson, Robert J. "Debunking the Digital Divide." *Newsweek* 25 Mar. 2002: 37.

Schuder, Rebecca. "Eagle Book Club." *Library Talk* Jan.–Feb. 2001: 17.

Schultz, Cynthia D. "Developing an Advocacy Plan for the School Library Media
   Center." *The Book Report* Nov.–Dec. 1999: 19–23.

Seelig, Fred. "Web Changes PR Industry." *Grand Rapids Business Journal* 24 Apr 2000:
   7–9.

Seewald, Jacqueline. "Advocacy Building Influence at the Grass Roots Level: Closing
   the School Year with Positive Public Relations." *The Book Report* May–June
   1999: 22–24.

Slowinski, Joe. "What Will the Future of Education Look Like?" *The Book Report*
   Jan.–Feb. 2002: 18–20.

Snyder, Timothy. *Getting Lead-Bottomed Administrators Excited about School Library
   Media Centers*. Libraries Unlimited, 2000.

United States Census Bureau. *United States Department of Commerce News*. 2 Feb.
   2002. 5 Mar. 2002 <.http://www.census.gov/mrts/www/current.html>.

Walters, Suzanne. "Marketing a How to Manual for Libraries." Neal-Schuman, 1992.

Wang, John. "Marketing Information for Small Businesses on the Web." *Fairfield
   County Business Journal* 24 June 1996: 13–15.

Wasman, Ann, comp. and ed. *Ideas for Promoting your School Library Media Program.* American Library Association, 1996.

Weingand, Darlene E. *Marketing/Planning Library Information Services.* Libraries Unlimited, 1999.

Winning Friends for the School Library: A PR Handbook. Linworth, 1994.

Wolfe, Lisa. *Library Public Relations, Promotions & Communications: a How-to-Do-It Manual.* Neal-Schuman, 1997.

Glossary

A

Adobe Acrobat Reader—creates a .pdf file format that retains the layout and design of the original document.

animated .gifs—a type of Graphic Interchange Format or an image that moves on a Web page.

AOL Instant Messenger—allows instant exchange of e-mail messages.

APA—American Psychological Association; format for documenting sources.

ask a librarian—online reference service.

B

banner—a Web page graphic that identifies a site or the content of a Web page.

book donation page—part of a home page that documents books donated by patrons to the library.

Bobby—a program that helps Web page designers check their pages for accessibility for persons with disabilities.

bookmark—an Internet site that is saved on your computer for later use (known as *Favorites* in Explorer).

broken links—links that do not connect to a Web site; some are temporarily unreachable links such as "network error," "sorry we have moved," or the host reorganizing its server, while others are links that connect to sites no longer in operation.

browsers—software that puts a graphical interface on the Internet; Explorer and Netscape are examples.

C

cell—a box in a spreadsheet or table where text is entered.

Chapter a Day Book Club—a reading incentive program that e-mails subscribers chapters of novels.

chat room—real-time discussion group on the Internet.

ClarisWorks—multimedia software program.

clear button—button on interactive form which is used to reset forms.

Colorado Study—conducted by Keith Curry Lance, Christine Hamilton-Pennell, and Marcie J. Rodney that shows a relationship between quality media programs and academic achievement.

Composer—a Web-authoring program included in Netscape.

D

design elements—features of a Web page that include the layout, fonts, images, color, and graphics.

digital divide—the gap between those who have access to the Internet and those who do not.

Dreamweaver—a Web-authoring program from Macromedia.

E

electronic pathfinder—guide to assisting students with their research that is published on a library's home page.

electronic stories—stories published on the Internet.

e-zine—electronic magazine that is published on the Internet.

F

FAQs—acronym for Frequently Asked Questions.

font—text in various styles and sizes.

Form Maker—software program for designing forms without learning .HTML tags.

frames—multiple sections of a Web page.

FrontPage—Web-authoring program from Microsoft.

G

.gif—Graphical Interface Format; file extension for an image.

H

home page—first page of a Web site; also called the index page.

hotlists—a list of Web pages used for student research.

.HTML—Hypertext Markup Language; the code used to write text for a Web page.

HyperStudio—multimedia authoring program from Knowledge Adventure.

I

image map—hyperlinks are placed within an image thus activating it, which when clicked, enable users to link to Web sites.

index page—first page of a Web site; also known as the home page.

interface—the means used to communicate with a computer or Internet.

Internet Explorer—Microsoft's browser.

J

.jpeg—Joint Photographic Experts Group; a file format for an image used for photographs.

L

link—creates a connection between one Internet site and another.

listserv—a computer program that automatically sends e-mail to everyone on a mailing list.

LM-NET—listserv for librarians.

logo—a graphic representation of a corporation or organization.

M

Majordomo—software program that directs e-mails to subscribers of a mailing list.

MLA—Modern Language Association.

multicolumn format—layout design for a Web page where each page is subdivided into two or more sections.

multimedia software—program that use text, audio, images, and videos such as PowerPoint and ClarisWorks.

N

navigational tool—allows a user to find their way through a Web site and includes backward and forward arrows.

netiquette—etiquette for e-mail and other forms of communication on the Internet.

Netscape—Internet browser.

Noodle Tools—software program that formats bibliographic citations.

O

OWL—Online Writing Lab of Purdue University.

P

Paint—a program used to draw images that can be used on the Internet.

.pdf—portable document format; a file format by Adobe Acrobat that enables the user to see documents such as brochures and newsletters exactly as designed.

plug-in—software that expands the capabilities of a browser allowing access to audio and video on the Internet.

PhotoShop—a graphic arts software program from Adobe.

pixels—picture element is unit of color that can be displayed on a computer monitor.

PowerPoint—a software program from Microsoft used for creating multimedia presentations.

Publisher—a software program from Microsoft used for creating brochures and newsletters.

R

read-in—a program designed to promote reading in which a community agrees to read the same book during a specific time period.

reservation calendar—online calendar used by teachers to schedule their classes in the library.

resolution—number of pixels that are displayed on a computer monitor.

response mechanism—method of determining readership of brochures, newsletters, and Web pages; examples are contests and surveys.

S

Section 508 Guidelines—amendment to the Rehabilitation Act of 1973 that requires that people with disabilities have equal access to electronic technology and information.

spam—unsolicited junk e-mail.

storyboard—a blueprint for visualizing the content of Web pages or presentations; a series of drawings arranged in order that shows the progression of a Web page.

T

Talk City—Internet site that enables users to set up a chat room.

template—a document with a pre-designed layout that can be copied and pasted to create new documents.

U

unplugged summer program—a library program that promotes reading by asking students to give up a week of watching television.

URL—Uniform Resource Locator or the address of a Web page.

V

video viewers—software programs that enable video to be transmitted and watched on the Internet.

virtual displays—online bulletin boards used for showcasing library events.

virtual reference desk—online reference service; also known as Ask a Librarian.

virus—a code that is put on your computer without your permission with the purpose of infecting your computer and causing harm to your programs.

W

Web-authoring program—software programs used for creating a home page such as FrontPage, Dreamweaver and Netscape Composer.

Webmaster—person who designs and maintains a home page.

Web page—a document found on the Internet; an Internet site.

Index

About the Authors

Ann Hill is a librarian at Washington Township High School in Sewell, New Jersey and a former social studies teacher. She received her BS from Penn State University, MEd from The College of New Jersey, and MLS from Rutgers University.

Julieta Dias Fisher was born in Mombasa, Kenya. She was raised and educated there as well as in India, Portugal, and the United States. She received her BA from American University and her MLS from Rowan University. Though she does not sport a bun, wear glasses or sensible shoes, she prefers the term librarian to media or instructional specialist! She has worked in academic, corporate, public, and school libraries.

Julieta and Ann are librarians in Washington Township High School in Sewell, New Jersey. They received the Winnebago Progressive School Award in 1999, for having the best school library in New Jersey, and have written several articles for *The Book Report* and *Library Talk*. They have conducted workshops for the New Jersey Education Association and the Educational Media Association of New Jersey.